E907 .K55 2012
The amateur :
33663004850505

DATE DUE

MAR 05 2013	
MAR 20 2013	

BRODART, CO.

Cat. No. 23-221

THE
AMATEUR

THE
AMATEUR

BARACK OBAMA IN THE WHITE HOUSE

EDWARD KLEIN

Since 1947
REGNERY
PUBLISHING, INC.
An Eagle Publishing Company • Washington, DC

Cataloging-in-Publication data on file with the Library of Congress
ISBN 978-1-59698-785-2

Published in the United States by
Regnery Publishing, Inc.
One Massachusetts Avenue NW
Washington, DC 20001
www.Regnery.com

Manufactured in the United States of America
10 9 8

Portions of chapter 15 first appeared in the *Huffington Post* in October 2010 as a five-part series written in collaboration with Richard Z. Chesnoff.

Lyrics of "Chicago (That Toddlin' Town)" by Fred Fisher, © Sony/ ATV Music Publishing LLC, Warner Chappell Music, Inc., EMI Music Publishing.

Books are available in quantity for promotional or premium use. Write to Director of Special Sales, Regnery Publishing, Inc., One Massachusetts Avenue NW, Washington, DC 20001, for information on discounts and terms, or call (202) 216-0600.

Distributed to the trade by
Perseus Distribution
387 Park Avenue South
New York, NY 10016

For Dolores, my courageous companion

CONTENTS

THE DARK SIDE
OF OBAMA

*Every man is a moon and has a [dark] side
which he turns toward nobody; you have to
slip around behind if you want to see it.*

—Mark Twain

This is a reporter's book.

During the past year and a half, I have interviewed nearly two hundred people, both inside and outside the White House. Many of these people have known Barack Obama for more than twenty years—from his earliest days in Chicago. Some of them were positive about Obama, others were negative, but the stories they told me had a remarkable consistency.

Bound in dozens of four-inch-thick three-ring notebooks, my transcribed notes run for almost a thousand pages and tell the story of a man who is at bottom temperamentally unsuited to be

the chief executive and commander in chief of the United States
of America. Here in these interviews we come face to face with
something new in American politics—*The Amateur*—a president
who is inept in the arts of management and governance, who
doesn't learn from his mistakes, and who therefore repeats policies that make our economy less robust and our nation less safe.
We discover a man who blames all his problems on those with
whom he disagrees ("Washington," "Republicans," "the media"),
who discards old friends and supporters when they are no longer
useful (Democrats, African-Americans, Jews), and who is so thin-
skinned that he constantly complains about what people say and
write about him. We come to know a strange kind of politician,
one who derives no joy from the cut and thrust of politics, but
who clings to the narcissistic life of the presidency.

This portrait of Obama is radically at odds with the image of
a centrist, pragmatic, post-partisan leader that his political handlers have tried to create. And it is a far cry from the Obama most
Americans remember from four years ago. Many of the people I
interviewed, including Republicans who voted against him, wondered what had happened to *that* Obama—the young, articulate
African-American senator who burst upon the political scene by
presenting himself as a new kind of politician, a peacemaker, a
mediator, and a conciliator who promised to heal the rift between
red and blue America?

Where did he vanish?

Did he ever exist?

Was he a figment of his own imagination, or of our imagination—or of both?

How did he turn out to be the most divisive president in recent American history?

Will Americans finally come to recognize the dark side of Barack Obama in the presidential election of 2012?

These are some of the critical questions I set out to answer in this book. My job as a reporter was complicated by the fact that Obama and his advisers have gone to elaborate lengths to hide his dark side. However, I have learned as a journalist that if you look long enough and hard enough and carefully enough, most truths are discoverable. As you will see in the pages that follow, I chose to launch my investigation in Chicago, where Obama first donned his disguise as an ideological wolf in sheep's clothing.

"Ever since I've known him, Obama has had delusions of grandeur and a preoccupation with his place in history," one of his oldest Chicago acquaintances told me. "He is afflicted with megalomania. How else can you explain the chutzpah of an obscure community organizer who began writing his autobiography before he was thirty years old—and before he had any accomplishments to write about? And how else can you explain the chutzpah of a first-term United States senator, who believed he was qualified for the most difficult job in the world—the presidency—even though he had never held a real job in his life?

"You can explain it with any number of words: arrogance, conceit, egotism, vanity, hubris," this person continued. "But whatever word you choose, it spells the same thing—disaster for the country he leads."

Obama's supporters claim that he has been falsely charged with being a leftwing ideologue. But based on my reporting, I concluded that Obama is actually *in revolt* against the values of the society he was elected to lead. Which is why he has refused to embrace American exceptionalism—the idea that Americans are a special people with a special destiny—and why he has railed at the capitalist system, demonized the wealthy, and embraced the Occupy Wall Street movement.

Of course, Obama doesn't see things that way. And therein lies the challenge for conservatives. As Peter Wehner, a senior fellow at the conservative Ethics and Public Policy Center, points out, "Barack Obama may be a lousy president... but he's a very good campaigner." He is determined to get reelected and go down in history books as a *transformative* president who turned America into a European-style democratic-socialist welfare state.

Shortly after Obama entered the White House, Treasury Secretary Tim Geithner warned him, "Your legacy is going to be preventing the second Great Depression."

To which Obama boasted, "That's not enough for me."

It may finally have become too much for the rest of us.

AS BILL SEES IT

CHAPPAQUA, NEW YORK, AUGUST 2011

Bill and Hillary were going at it again, fighting tooth and nail over their favorite subject: *themselves*.

It was a warm summer Sunday—a full year away from the 2012 Democratic National Convention—and Bill Clinton was urging Hillary to think the unthinkable. He wanted her to challenge Barack Obama for their party's presidential nomination. No American politician had attempted to usurp a sitting president of his own party since Ted Kennedy failed to unseat Jimmy Carter more than thirty years before.

"Why risk everything now?" Hillary demanded to know.

"Because," Bill replied, "the country *needs* you!"

His voice was several decibels louder than necessary, and his nose was turning shades of red.

"The country needs *us*!" he shouted, banging a fist on his desk to drive home his point.

"The timing's not right," Hillary shot back.

Unlike Bill, she didn't raise her voice, but her face was flushed and her eyes were bulging, which often happened when Bill tried to force her to do something she didn't want to do.

"I want my term [at the State Department] to be an important one, and running away from it now would leave it as a footnote," Hillary said. "I want to make my mark as a statesman. Anyway, I'm young enough to wait my turn and run [for the White House] in the next cycle."

"I know *you're* young enough!" Bill said, raising his voice yet another notch. "That's not what I'm worried about. I'm worried that *I'm* not young enough."

They were seated in Bill's home office in the converted red barn located a few short steps away from their Dutch Colonial house on 15 Old House Lane in Chappaqua, a suburb of New York City. The barn walls were lined with books on history and politics, with a good smattering of biographies. Beneath the high, long windows were souvenirs from Bill's travels—a cigar store Indian, African bows and arrows, and a spear. Outside, four black Secret Service SUVs—two for the former president and two for the secretary of state—cooked under the August sun.

Like so many of the verbal brawls the Clintons had engaged in down through the years, this one had a theatrical quality about it, as though it was being staged for an audience. And, in fact, their quarrel was taking place in front of a few old friends who were both fascinated and appalled by the fierce spectacle.

Later, one of those witnesses would recall for this book: "The argument about her running had been going on for days, if not for weeks, and Hillary was clearly exasperated with Bill. He wouldn't take 'No' for an answer. There was a reason Bill didn't want to wait until the next presidential cycle, in 2016, when Hillary'll be sixty-nine and Bill'll be seventy. Bill's had a lot of serious health setbacks—quadruple bypass surgery, a collapsed lung, two coronary stents—and all that's left him feeling like he's living on borrowed time."

In the middle of their argument, Hillary's BlackBerry went off and she answered it. Bill kept right on talking over her phone conversation. Then Hillary's other BlackBerry rang, and she picked that one up, too, and placed it against her other ear, and now she was talking into two phones at once, making important decisions about foreign policy, but Bill continued to argue with her, and she looked really pissed; she made a throat-cutting motion for him to shut up.

When she hung up, Bill began to rattle off the results of a secret poll in which potential voters had been asked how they would feel about Hillary's making a run against Obama for the White House in 2012.

"Your poll numbers are all positive," Bill said, pacing the floor. "African-Americans are moving away from Obama and in your direction. Latinos, too. And Jews. Women and the elderly are all on your side. Young college boys are the only ones clinging to Obama. It's a no-brainer. You can win if you want back in the White House as much as I do."

A cloud passed over Hillary's face. "Is it going to get out that you did this poll?" she asked.

Everyone in the room instantly grasped the implication of her question: Would Barack Obama find out about Bill's act of political treachery?

"Nobody's going to find out about it," Bill assured her.

Hillary gave him a skeptical look; she didn't have to be told that lying came easily to her husband.

"All of us in the room, including Hillary, assumed that Bill had commissioned the poll, although he didn't specifically say so," said one of their friends. "Of course, he could have been bluffing. That would be like him. Hillary has said many times that he plays liar's poker even with her. He can't help himself. The odd thing was that he didn't have a bound notebook with the results. He just reeled off the number from his head. But that's like him, too. He has an amazing ability to remember details of policy."

———————

Hillary was seated in a leather chair, stroking her toy poodle, Tally, perched on her lap. Bill's chocolate lab, Seamus, was roaming around the room, and at one point Tally leapt off Hillary's lap and chased Seamus out of the barn. Everyone laughed, breaking the tension.

But then Bill picked up the quarrel again, and he and Hillary were going at it full throttle when Chelsea showed up. She was alone, without her husband, Marc Mezvinsky. With her long, flowing blonde hair and stylish weekend outfit, she was the picture of a confident 31-year-old career woman. And in fact, Chelsea had recently joined the board of Barry Diller's Internet media holding company IAC/InterActive Corp, and was in secret negotiations with Steve Capus, the president of NBC News, to become a special on-air correspondent.

Chelsea greeted her parents' guests with a broad smile, but she looked pained to find her parents arguing with each other. She asked her mother to step outside, and they walked across the stone patio to the fenced-in swimming pool, where they could be seen engaging in animated conversation.

When they returned, Chelsea made it clear that she had come down on her father's side of the argument: she wanted her mother to challenge Obama in the Democratic primaries.

Chelsea was still smarting from the results of the 2008 primary campaign, in which her mother racked up eighteen million votes and actually beat Obama in the popular vote, but lost to him chiefly because of the votes of super delegates. Chelsea wanted to wreak revenge against Obama's campaign operatives who had dissed her mother and tried to paint her father as a racist.

"You *deserve* to be president," Chelsea told her mother.

Bill agreed, and he said he might be able to persuade others to commission their own polls, matching up Hillary against Obama.

"What are you trying to do—force my hand?" Hillary said.

"I want everyone to know how strong you poll," Bill said.

"Go ahead and knock yourself out," Hillary said, shrugging.

Bill started to think out loud about political strategy. Maybe he would leak some of the findings in the poll. Or, alternatively, he could roll out the results of the poll to a media organization. He had friends at NBC News; he could trust that network. That's why he had steered Chelsea to Steve Capus, the president of NBC's news division. The important thing, he concluded, was getting out the poll's main finding—namely, that while Obama's numbers were in the toilet, Hillary was the most popular politician in America.

Listening to Bill Clinton, the master politician of his age, soliloquize about politics was an awesome experience, and everyone in the barn, including Hillary, hung on his every word.

Bill flashed a sheepish smile as he revealed that he had spent the past year writing a book about how to put America back to work. In his book, he intended to take some serious shots at Obama's jobs and tax proposals. He thought Obama had made a huge mistake by attacking Wall Street executives, many of whom were Bill's personal friends and had pledged to pay more taxes to help cut the deficit.

"The economy's a mess, it's dead flat," he said. "America has lost its Triple-A rating. Hillary, you have years of experience on Obama. You know better than Obama does, and far better than those guys who are advising him. They don't know what they're doing. They govern in sound bites. You'd be the *ideal* candidate. You'd..."

He paused for a moment, as if a new thought had suddenly occurred to him.

"If you become president, will we have to build a second Clinton library?" he asked.

"You bet," Hillary said, smiling for the first time.

"Listen," Bill continued, "you can't be blamed for the economy. People think of you as tough, experienced, and tested. You could defeat any Republican nominee better than Obama and keep control of Congress, or at least not bleed as many seats as Obama'll bleed the party next year. The voters remember how they were better off when we were in the White House. *You* could fix the economy. *We* could fix it if *we*... I mean if *you* were president."

Hillary rolled her eyes.

"I'm the highest-ranking member in Obama's cabinet," she pointed out. "I eat breakfast with the guy every Thursday morning. What about loyalty, Bill? What about *loyalty*?"

"Loyalty is a joke," Bill said. "Loyalty doesn't exist in politics. There's no such word in the political rulebook. I've had two successors since I left the White House—Bush and Obama—and I've heard more from Bush, asking for my advice, than I've heard from Obama. I have no relationship with the president—none whatsoever. Obama doesn't know how to be president. He doesn't know how the world works. He's incompetent. He's... he's..."

Bill's voice was growing hoarse—he was speaking in a rough whisper—but he looked as though he could go on forever bashing Obama. And then, all at once and without warning, he stopped cold.

He bit his lower lip and scanned the faces in the room. He was plainly gratified to see that his audience was spellbound. They were waiting for the politician par excellence to deliver his final judgment on the forty-fourth president of the United States.

"Barack Obama," said Bill Clinton, "is an amateur!"

PART I

CHICAGO, THAT TODDLIN' TOWN

Chicago, Chicago that toddlin' town
Chicago, Chicago I will show you around—I love it
Bet your bottom dollar you lose the blues in
Chicago, Chicago
The town that Billy Sunday could not shut down

—"Chicago (That Toddlin' Town)"
by Fred Fisher

CHAPTER 1

HOLLOW AT THE CORE

Whether he knew of this deficiency himself I can't say. I think the knowledge came to him at last— only at the very last.... I think it had whispered to him things about himself which he did not know, things of which he had no conception till he took counsel with this great solitude—and the whisper had proved irresistibly fascinating. It echoed loudly within him because he was hollow at the core.

—Joseph Conrad, *Heart of Darkness*

Of all the Chicago people I interviewed, none got to know Barack Obama quite the way David Scheiner, MD, did. Scheiner was Obama's personal physician for twenty-two years— from the mid-1980s, when Obama was a community organizer, until he was elected president of the United States.

Today, at the age of seventy-three, Dr. Scheiner is a rail-thin, spunky, unreconstructed old lefty. He belongs to Physicians for a National Health Program, a far-leftwing organization that lobbies for single-payer national health insurance—or, in Dr. Scheiner's own words, "socialized medicine." He had great hopes for

Obama in the White House, because when Obama was his patient he made no secret of the fact that he favored the kind of socialized medicine that is practiced in Canada and Western Europe.

Given Dr. Scheiner's leftist leanings, I expected him to be a champion of his former patient. To my surprise, however, he turned out to be one of Obama's most severe and unforgiving critics.

"I look at his healthcare program and I can't see how it can work," Scheiner said. "He has no cost control. There would be no effective cost control in his program. The [Congressional Budget Office] said it's going to be incredibly expensive... and the thing that I really am worried about is, if it is the failure that I think it would be, then health reform will be set back a long, long time.

"When Barack Obama planned this health program, he didn't include on his healthcare team anyone who actually practiced medicine in the trenches the way I do," Dr. Scheiner continued. "I'm an old-fashioned doctor. I still make house calls. I still use the first black bag that I got out of medical school. My patients have my home phone number. It's true that Dr. Ezekiel Emanuel, the brother of Rahm Emanuel, was on the healthcare team, but Ezekiel is a medical oncologist, not a general physician."

Dr. Scheiner's grievances against Obama went well beyond Obama's policies to the very nature of the man.

"My main objection to Barack Obama is that he is a great speaker and a lousy communicator," Dr. Scheiner said. "He isn't getting his message across to people. He isn't showing that he really cares. To this day he hasn't communicated with members of Congress.

"He's got academic University of Chicago-type people around him who don't care. Where is our Surgeon General, the obese Dr. Regina Benjamin? Why hasn't *she* said anything during this healthcare debate? Ronald Reagan had C. Everett Koop as his surgeon general. Believe me, Regina Benjamin is no Everett Koop. In fact, Obama's whole cabinet has been a disappointment. Health and Human Services Secretary Kathleen Sebelius is a joke."

I asked Dr. Scheiner why he thought Obama had been such a dismal failure as president. He thought for a moment, then said:

"I can really relate to people, but I never really related to him. I never had the closeness with him that I had with other patients. It was a purely professional relationship. He was always gracious and polite. But I never really connected to him. He was distant. When I think of why he's had problems in the White House, I think there is too much of the University of Chicago in him. By which I mean he's academic, lacks passion and feeling, and doesn't have the sense of humanity that I expected.

"Obama has an academic detachment," he continued. "I treat many patients from the University of Chicago faculty, and I've been able to crack through their academic detachment. Not Obama. We never got to the point where we'd discuss intimate things. For instance I never heard anything about his family life. Other patients invited me to dinner and their homes, but Obama never did. Obama invited his barber to his inauguration—his *barber!* But *I* wasn't invited. Believe me, that hurt."

CHAPTER 2

A GHOSTLY PRESENCE

---

*It's not about charisma and personality,
it's about results...*

—Steve Jobs

One morning in the spring of 1991, a telephone rang in Gannett House, a white, Greek Revival-style building that serves as the headquarters of the *Harvard Law Review*, the prestigious student-run journal of legal scholarship. The caller was Douglas Baird, dean of the University of Chicago Law School. He was looking for Barack Obama, who had gained national fame as "the first black president of the *Review*."

Actually, Obama was not the first person of color to be president of the *Review*. That distinction belonged to Raj Marphatia, who was born and raised in Bombay (now known as Mumbai),

India, and who had become the *Review*'s president four years earlier. But while Marphatia's presidency went largely unnoticed, Obama's attracted a great deal of attention in the liberal mainstream media. That publicity, in turn, led to a publishing contract for a book on race relations and several offers of prestigious clerkships and lucrative jobs. The liberal world was already beating a path to Barack Obama's door.

"I made a cold call to the *Harvard Law Review* and spoke to Barack," recalled Baird, who is no longer the dean of the Chicago Law School but is still a member of its faculty. "I asked him, 'Do you have an interest in teaching law?' and he said, 'No. My plan is to write a book on voting rights.' And I said, 'Why don't you write that book here at the University of Chicago. I can give you an office and a word processor and make you a Visiting Law and Government Fellow.'

"He accepted," Baird continued, "and several months after he arrived, he came to my office and said, 'Boss'—he called me boss—'that book I told you about—well, it's taken a slightly different direction. It's my autobiography.' I was astonished. He was all of thirty years old and he was writing his autobiography!"

For the next twelve years, Obama taught at the Law School—first as a Lecturer, then as a Senior Lecturer. He earned about $60,000 a year and was given an office, a secretary, and health benefits. He was, by all accounts, a ghostly presence on the faculty—rarely seen and virtually never heard from.

"You just never saw him at a lunch or at a workshop," said Richard Epstein, who was made interim dean of the Law School in 2001, while Obama was still there. "I did not see any signs of intellectual curiosity or power. He did not have a way of listening to you that drew you in. But it was rarely the case that you could figure out what he thought. An inaccurate story was published that claimed Obama was given a tenured offer to join the faculty. But it never came to the faculty for approval. How could you make a tenured offer to a man who had never written a scholarly article?

"At the time," Epstein continued, "Obama saw himself as a serious intellectual, which he definitely was not. His course was very popular and he was an engaging teacher, but not one with a serious academic set of interests. The members of the faculty reserved a round table for ten in the Quadrangle Club, where we had lunch and engaged in an intense intellectual exchange. We had a no-sports and no-politics rule and a single-topic rule. Everybody bashed everybody. You put yourself once more into the breach and prepared to have the guillotine come down on your head.

"But Barack Obama never attended these lunches. I firmly believe that his systematic withdrawal from engagement with other members of the faculty stemmed from his not wanting to put himself at intellectual risk. He was always a political actor with many irons in the fire."

———

Interestingly enough, Douglas Baird—the man who hired Obama—had a slightly different take on Obama than Richard Epstein.

"I should also say that, like Richard, I'd have liked it if Barack had been more involved," Baird said. "But that wasn't what he was about. He was spending his time as a law lecturer, a member of a law firm, and a writer. He was an excellent teacher. I had access to his teacher evaluations. The students loved him. He was a charismatic figure.

"Of course, I grant you that it's one thing to be a charismatic figure and walk into a room and excite students, and quite another thing to be a leader—to hire people, motivate people, and manage decision-making. That's not something Barack experienced or learned at the Chicago Law School. I know people in the White house, and I don't get a sense from my conversations with them that there's anything in Barack's experience as a law professor that prepared him for the leadership part of the presidential job."

CHAPTER 3

"YOU KEEP OUT OF THIS!"

A fanatic is a man that does what he thinks th' Lord wud do if He knew th' facts iv th' case.

—Finley Peter Dunne, *Mr. Dooley*

In 1996, while he was still teaching law, Barack Obama was elected to the Illinois Senate. During most of his seven years in the state capital of Springfield, the Republicans were in the majority, and as was his custom at the University of Chicago, Obama was conspicuous by his absence.

"He hardly showed up at all," said Laura Anderson, who at the time served as deputy chief of staff to the Republican leader of the Senate. "He didn't even show up for picture day, and he didn't go to committee. He had no interest in the process, or in learning the process of being a good senator. He had no interest in government itself. He just wanted to stand on the Senate floor and give speeches."

Obama did, however, have an interest in opposing a law that would have banned late-term partial birth abortions, a gruesome procedure that was once condemned by the late New York Senator Daniel Patrick Moynihan as "too close to infanticide." All across the state of Illinois, people were riveted by the controversial debate. The *Chicago Sun-Times* ran a cartoon showing God reaching down from heaven to a baby in front of Obama, who is holding a sign that reads "Live Birth Abortions" and yelling at God, "You keep out of this!"

Courtesy of *Chicago Sun-Times* / Jack Higgins

An Illinois nurse named Jill Stanek testified before the Health and Human Services Committee that she had discovered that babies were being aborted alive and allowed to die in soiled utility rooms.

One baby was accidentally thrown into the trash. Though Obama never showed up at the committee hearings, he voted against the bill—not once, but twice.

When, after a decade in the political wilderness, Illinois Democrats gained a majority in the legislature, Obama became chairman of the Health and Human Services Committee. As chairman, he prevented the "Live Baby Bill" from getting a committee hearing, guaranteeing that the legislation would die, much as the late-term babies were dying in the state's hospitals.

CHAPTER 4

"YOU SHOULD KNOW BETTER WHEN POLITICIANS MAKE PROMISES"

Almost by definition, charismatic leaders are unpredictable, for they are bound by neither tradition nor rules; they are not answerable to other human beings.

—Eileen Barker, *New Religious Movements*

Obama always believed he was destined for great things, and after a few short years as a state senator, he felt frustrated and eager to move on. And so, in 2000, against the advice of his wife, friends, and colleagues, he challenged Bobby Rush, a former Black Panther and four-term member of the House of Representatives, for Rush's seat from Chicago's black South Side.

During the Democratic primary, most African-American political leaders stuck by Rush, who treated his upstart opponent with
contempt, once remarking, "Barack Obama went to Harvard and
became an educated fool."

Rush walloped Obama, winning the primary by a margin of
two to one. "[Obama] was blinded by his ambition," Rush said
later. "Obama has never suffered from a lack of believing that
he can accomplish whatever he decides to try. Obama believes
in Obama."

After Obama's humiliating defeat, he was broke and deeply
in debt, and it looked as though he might be finished in public
life. For a narcissist like Obama, this was a calamitous turn of
events, and during the dark days that followed his defeat, he
turned to Michelle for comfort. But she was in no mood to offer
him sympathy. After all, he had refused to listen to her warnings
about taking on the formidable Bobby Rush. He had put his family in a precarious financial position. And he had dashed Michelle's
hopes of creating a stable and secure future. As a result, their
marriage was on the rocks, and Obama confided to friends that
he and Michelle were talking about divorce.

"Michelle actually had divorce papers drawn up," one of her
friends told me.

Obama was so depressed that some of his friends worried
that he was suicidal. One day, while he was playing basketball
at the East Bank Club, a vast fitness center and Chicago institution, Obama was approached by Jim Reynolds, the co-founder
and CEO of Loop Capital Markets, a global investment firm,

and a mover and shaker in Chicago's wealthy African-American community.

"Is this you?" Reynolds asked, holding up a copy of Obama's memoir, *Dreams from My Father*.

"Yeah," Obama replied.

"Let's go and have a cup of coffee," Reynolds said.

Over coffee, Obama bared his soul. He told Reynolds that Michelle was "kicking my butt," and he didn't know what his next move should be.

"What do you want to do?" Reynolds asked.

"I don't want to be a burden to my wife," Obama said. "I want to make her proud. But no matter what, I'm determined to be successful in politics. I want to go national. I want to run for the United States Senate."

"Come hang with me," Reynolds said. "I know a couple of people. I'll introduce you around town."

Obama's meeting with Jim Reynolds was a decisive turning point in his political career, for it marked the beginning of his relationship with Chicago's African-American moneyed elite. As we shall see, this relationship would blossom for several years, then turn sour, degenerating into bitterness, rancor, and resentment.

―――――

Early in his campaign for the United States Senate, Obama appeared at the offices of *N'DIGO,* Chicago's leading African-American magazine. Only months before, Hermene Hartman,

N'DIGO's dynamic founder and publisher, had put Obama on the cover of her magazine—a first for the state senator. This time, however, Obama was looking for more than mere publicity. He desperately needed money to fund his campaign.

"He came to me and said, 'I need you to raise $50,000 for me,'" Hartman recalled in an interview for this book. "I said, 'You're out of your mind. I don't have $50,000, and if I did, I wouldn't give it to you.' And he said, 'But I gotta get it. I opened up an office, turned the phones on, the lights are on, and I gotta move forward. C'mon, think of something.'

"He said, 'I've got one more shot,'" Hartman continued. "Michelle's going to kill me." He couldn't tell Michelle that he had gone ahead and secretly opened an office even though they didn't have any money. He knew that she would be furious. She was fed up and wasn't going to take it anymore. He had to be successful. It was do or die.

"So I called a friend named Al Johnson, who was the first African-American to have a General Motors dealership," Hartman went on. "Al, who's now deceased, was a political player, a supporter of politicians, and he had his own political action committee. I said, 'Al, I have a wonderful person I want you to meet and support.' And Al met Barack at the East Bank Club. Afterward, Al called me and said, 'We hit it off. I gave your boy $50,000. I think he's going to go far.'

"Now, in Chicago, 'far' is the mayor's office," Hartman went on. "And I said to Al, 'I don't see Barack in the mayor's office. This is a national guy. He can cross over and appeal to both blacks and whites.'"

In addition to being the publisher of *N'DIGO*, Hermene Hartman is also the past president of the Alliance of Business Leaders and Entrepreneurs, a powerful group of African-Americans in Chicago. The members of ABLE, as the group is known, were the first to get behind Obama's bid for the United States Senate.

"Barack was launched by black business people," Hartman told me. "I call them Day One People. Jim Reynolds, who had met Barack on the basketball court and introduced him around, held a fundraiser for him in his living room. The next day, Barack called me to ask, 'How did I do?' I said, 'You sounded like you're running for dogcatcher.' And he said, 'What do you mean?' I said, 'If you're running for United States senator, you have to broaden your view beyond neighborhood concerns. You have to go sit with Jesse Jackson. He knows these subjects—Africa, Europe, the whole international scene.'

"So I called Jesse and said, 'Barack needs to talk to you. He needs some broadening.' And Jesse said, 'Sure, I'll meet with him.' Barack lived not far from Jesse's Operation PUSH [People United to Save Humanity], and for the next year Jesse invited Barack to speak at PUSH every Saturday so that he could hone his speaking skills."

Perhaps out of fear of alienating white voters, Obama never acknowledged his debt to Jesse Jackson. Nor, for that matter, did

Obama show much gratitude to the many other African-Americans who had helped him ascend from obscurity to national acclaim. As Hartman put it to me: "Barack is not necessarily known for his loyalty."

A particularly egregious case in point was Obama's treatment of Steven Rogers, an African-American who made a fortune in the private sector before becoming the Gund Family Distinguished Professor of Entrepreneurship at Northwestern University's Kellogg School of Management.

"I first met Obama at a golf fundraiser for a charter school on the West Side of Chicago, which serves predominantly African-American students from low-income families," Rogers told me. "He was an unexpected addition to my foursome, who repeatedly talked to me about his desire to run for the United States Senate. I asked him, 'What do you want from me?' He said, 'My wife will not allow me to run for the Senate until I clear up the debts from my unsuccessful run for Congress.' I believe he told me that he had $8,000 of [private] debt. I donated $3,000.

"After that meeting," Rogers continued, "he began leaving messages on my cell phone, asking for money for his campaign and that of other Democrats, such as Senator Tom Daschle. He told me that he wanted to show the Democratic Party leaders that he could raise money for candidates throughout the country, and that his success in doing so would increase his chances for being appointed to a powerful Senate committee, such as Finance. He specifically asked that I donate $2,000 to five Democrats who were running for reelection.

"I agreed to make the campaign contributions, and I invited him to address my students, which he did. Afterwards, in the parking lot, I asked him, 'Where are you going next?' He said, 'Man, I'm going to the South Side. Every Saturday I've got to see Reverend [Jesse] Jackson.' And I said, 'When you get elected to the Senate, I want you to come back here and speak to my students.' And he said, 'I'll tell you what. When I get elected, I'll bring your students to Washington.' I said, 'Don't bother. Just bring your black butt back here.'

"After he got elected, my students tried to contact him. He wouldn't answer their calls. So I called and said, 'Listen, Senator, I'd like you to come.' And he said, 'Listen, Steve, I can't come. I'm just inundated with requests. I have governors calling me. I have Warren Buffett calling me.' I said, 'What about that money I gave you?' And he said, 'Come on, man, you should know better when politicians make promises.'

"I was furious, and I said, 'You're a dirty, rotten motherfucker. What kind of shit are you trying to pull? Fuck you, you big-eared motherfucker. You said you'd bring the Kellogg students to Washington, and all I'm asking is that you come speak to your constituents.'

"A year later, he finally showed up. He gave a powerful speech. He took pictures with my wife and me. And I haven't spoken to him since. What you have with Barack Obama is a lack of character."

CHAPTER 5

THE MAN WHO PREPARED OBAMA FOR THE PRESIDENCY

The true fanatic is a theocrat, someone who sees himself as acting on behalf of some super-personal force: the Race, the Party, History, the Proletariat, the Poor, and so on. These absolve him from evil, hence he may safely do anything in their service.

—Lloyd Billingsley, *Religion's Rebel Son*

66 I bring you greetings from my pastor, the Reverend Jeremiah Wright."

For years, that was the way Barack Obama began his speeches when he appeared before black church groups all across America. By the time he became a United States senator and set out to run for president, Obama even *sounded* a lot like Jeremiah Wright. He had dropped his professorial manner of speaking and adopted Wright's rhythmic cadences—his use of homey idioms, his pregnant pauses between phrases, and his rhetorical technique of creating a call-and-response pattern from the audience, which was aimed at whipping his listeners into a state of euphoria. (Obama employed this oratorical technique to great effect in the 2008 presidential campaign.)

Until Obama married Michelle Robinson in 1991, when he was thirty years old, his most significant adult relationship was with Jeremiah Wright. His connection to Wright ran long and deep, and went back further than has been generally reported. It started well before Obama joined Wright's congregation, Trinity United Church of Christ, where the pastor's sermons on Black Liberation Theology encouraged a victimization mentality among his black parishioners.

When Jeremiah Wright and Trinity made headlines during the 2008 presidential race, most white Americans had never heard of Black Liberation Theology. According to Anthony B. Bradley, an associate professor of theology at The King's College in New York City, Black Liberation Theology asserts "life for blacks in America has been in the past and will be in the future a life of being victimized by the oppression of whites. In today's terms, it is the conviction that, forty years after the Civil Rights Act, conditions for blacks have not substantially changed...."

"One of the pillars of Obama's home church, Trinity United Church of Christ, is 'economic parity,'" Professor Bradley continues. "On its website, Trinity claims that God is not pleased with 'America's economic mal-distribution.' Among all of the controversial comments by Jeremiah Wright, the idea of massive wealth redistribution is the most alarming. The code language 'economic parity' and references to 'mal-distribution' is nothing more than channeling the twisted economic views of Karl Marx. Black Liberation theologians have explicitly stated a preference for Marxism as an ethical framework for the black church because Marxist thought is predicated on a system of oppressor class (whites) versus victim class (blacks)."

Echoes of Jeremiah Wright's Marxist ideology can be found in many of Obama's remarks. For instance, when Obama says, "I think when you spread the wealth around, it's good for everybody," he is channeling Jeremiah Wright. This should come as no surprise, since Wright's influence on Obama was unrivaled for more than twenty years. And those were Obama's formative years when his core beliefs took shape. Not even Michelle Obama held such intellectual and political sway over her husband.

Jeremiah Wright became far more than a religious and spiritual guide to Obama; he was his substitute father, life coach, and political inspiration wrapped in one package. At each step of Obama's career, Wright was there with practical advice and counsel. Wright encouraged Obama to make a career of politics, and he offered to hook up Obama with members of Trinity United Church of Christ who had money and important connections. After Obama lost the congressional election to Bobby Rush and Michelle talked about divorcing him, a despondent Obama went to Wright for help. "Pick yourself up!" Wright exhorted him. "Pick yourself up!"

It would be no exaggeration to say that Jeremiah Wright was the person who fulfilled Obama's father-hunger, repaired his fractured ego, and prepared him to run for president.

Neither Obama nor Jeremiah Wright has ever told the full story of how they came together. In the summer of 1985—four years before he met Michelle and seven years before he married her—Obama approached the Reverend Lacy Kirk "L. K." Curry to seek his help in organizing black churches in Chicago's African-American communities. Curry was the legendary minister of the Emmanuel Baptist Church and the president of Chicago's Inter-denominational Ministerial Alliance, where Jeremiah Wright had once been a member of the board of directors. Obama struck Curry as cocksure and overconfident, and he told the young community organizer, "You know what your problem is, young man? You need to know a preacher who knows more than you do. You need to go talk to Jeremiah Wright."

And so that summer, Obama went to see Wright, whose sermons, in the words of David Mendell, one of Obama's early biographers, "sometimes more [resembled] left-wing political rants than religious preaching."

"What I remember," Wright said when I asked him about his first meeting with Obama, "is that he came to talk to me as a community organizer, not in search of Christ. I said what Joseph's brothers in the Bible said when they saw him coming across the field: 'Behold this dreamer!' Barack came to me with this dream, man. He wasn't from Chicago and he was gonna organize all these different churches—Catholic churches and black churches— on Chicago's far South Side. And I'm saying, 'You can't organize the black churches. You don't *know* the black church. Listen, man, we got Baptists who won't speak to Presbyterians 'cause they don't immerse. We got Church of God and Christ who don't speak to Baptists because they don't speak in tongues. You ain't gonna organize no churches.'"

My interview with Wright, who, at seventy years of age, is retired from the pulpit at Trinity, took place on a bleak November morning in his current office on the campus of the Kwame Nkrumah Academy, a charter school that is named after the late Marxist dictator of the West African nation of Ghana. Since retiring, Wright has moved from his modest quarters in Trinity's parsonage to a new million-dollar mansion along a golf course in the posh Tinley Park section of Chicago.

As might be imagined, I had serious reservations about meeting with Wright, whose vitriolic sermons demonizing white people and portraying the United States as evil had turned him into a pariah in most parts of America. Yet, I discovered that despite Wright's dreadful excesses, his harebrained ideas, and his outright bigotry, he was still respected in large swaths of Chicago's African-American community, where he was admired as a biblical scholar and prophetic minister. My friends in that community urged me to swallow my reservations about Wright and meet with him.

"Go listen to what Dr. Wright has to say," one friend told me. "You're a journalist and Wright has a story that's a real eye-opener. It'll cast a whole new light on Obama's clumsy, crude, and *amateurish* handling of the greatest crisis in his political career, his public renunciation of the man he once referred to as 'like my father'—Jeremiah Wright."

"After Barack and I got to know each other, it got to the point where he would just drop by my church to talk," Wright said. "And the talk gradually moved away from his community-organizing concerns—street cleaning, housing, child care, and those kinds of needs—to larger things, more personal things. Like trying to make sense of the world. Like trying to make sense out of the diverse racial and religious background from which he came. He was confused. He wanted to know who he was.

"And I told him, 'Well, you already know the Muslim piece of your background,'" Wright continued. "'You studied Islam, didn't you?' And Barack said, 'Yeah, Rev, I studied Islam. But help me understand Christianity, because I already know Islam.' And I said, 'Well, let's start from the beginning. Who do you say Jesus is? Let's boil it down to the basics.'"

"Did you convert Obama from Islam to Christianity?" I asked Wright.

"That's hard to tell," Wright replied. "I think I convinced him that it was okay for him to make a choice in terms of who he believed Jesus is. And I told him it was really okay and not a putdown of the Muslim part of his family or his Muslim friends."

As a result of his stirring, primetime keynote speech at the 2004 Democratic National Convention, Obama became an overnight celebrity. His memoir, *Dreams from My Father*, which had languished on remainder piles in bookstores, rocketed to the top of the *New York Times* bestseller list. Suddenly wealthy (his current net worth is estimated at $10.5 million), he and Michelle donated $22,500 to Trinity United Church of Christ in 2006. The following year, as he prepared to throw his hat into the presidential ring, he was still a Trinity congregant, and sometimes attended services where Wright delivered poisonous sermons against whites, Jews, and America.

Why did Obama remain a member of Trinity?

Did he agree with what Wright said from the pulpit?

And if not, how could he sit there and listen to such rubbish?

"How [can we] reconcile this church membership... with the fact of [Obama's] own family—his white mother, grandmother, and grandfather?" Shelby Steele wrote in *A Bound Man*, his brilliant analysis of Obama's racial identity. "It was not a 'Black Value System' that prepared Obama so well for the world. Nor was it 'black community' or 'black family.' It was not black anything. One could easier argue that his good luck was to be born into a white 'family,' 'community,' and 'value system.' And, in fact, isn't his success, his ease in the American mainstream, due more to assimilation than to blackness? Isn't his great advantage over other blacks precisely his exposure from infancy on to mainstream culture? And doesn't it then follow that *assimilation* might be a very reasonable strategy for black uplift? And, correspondingly, doesn't Obama's success make the precise point that 'blackness' is a dead end?"

When it comes to dealing with the inconvenient truth about Barack Obama's deep-rooted relationship with Jeremiah Wright,

liberals have struggled to find a way to absolve Obama from cul-
pability. Some liberals argue that "buppies" (young, black urban
professionals) like Obama flocked to Sunday services at Trinity in
order to assuage their feelings of guilt about being better off than
the majority of their fellow African-Americans. Sitting in the pews
of Trinity, they could shout *Amen, brother!* when Wright declared:
"How do I tell my children about the African Jesus who is not the
guy they see in the picture of the blond-haired, blue-eyed guy in
their Bible or the figment of white supremacists [sic] imagination
that they see in Mel Gibson's movies?"

According to Salim Muwakkil, a Chicago journalist, Wright
"had the reputation of a militant guy who provided kind of
vicarious militance for Chicago's black elites. So they could get a
dose of militance on Sunday and go back home and feel pretty
good about doing their part for the black movement."

Other liberals have come up with a different theory to explain
how Obama could sit week after week in a church that preached
white wickedness and black superiority. They argue that it was
Michelle Obama, not Barack, who chose Trinity because she
wanted to associate with what *Washington Post* columnist Eugene
Robinson, in his book *Disintegration: The Splintering of Black
America*, termed "a small Transcendent [black] elite with such
enormous wealth, power, and influence that even white folks have
to genuflect."

But Jeremiah Wright didn't buy any of these explanations.

"Brides like to have their weddings at a church, which is why
I think Michelle came to Trinity," Wright told me. "That's been
my sneaking suspicion, because Michelle didn't belong to any

church when she married Barack. Where have you heard or read about her family raising her in church? My point is—and I haven't said this publicly to anybody before—but like you talk about Toni Morrison, you talk about Maya Angelou, you talk about these black women, they grew up in a church, most of them. Michelle didn't. She grew up in a kind of Jack and Jill middle income, completely middle-class environment.

"And even after Barack and Michelle came to the church," Wright went on, "their kids weren't raised in the church like you raise other kids in Sunday school. No. Church is not their thing. It never was their thing. Michelle was not the kind of black woman whose momma made her go to church, made her go to Sunday school, made her go to B.Y.P.U [Baptist Young People's Union]. She wasn't raised in that kind of environment. So the church was not an integral part of their spiritual lives after they got married.

"But"—and here Wright paused for emphasis—"the church *was* an integral part of Barack's *politics*. Because he needed that black base."

The conflict between church and state—between Jeremiah Wright's racist brand of religion and Barack Obama's "post-racial" brand of politics—came to an inevitable head on February 9, 2007. That was the day before Obama planned to launch his presidential campaign from the steps of the Old State Capitol in Springfield, Illinois—a move aimed at associating himself with

Springfield's most famous citizen, Abraham Lincoln. Wright was scheduled to deliver the invocation, but several days before the event, *Rolling Stone* magazine published a devastating profile of Barack Obama's minister.

"Wright takes the pulpit here one Sunday and solemnly, sonorously declares that he will recite ten essential facts about the United States," the *Rolling Stone* piece said.

> "Fact number one: We've got more black men in prison than there are in college," he intones. "Fact number two: Racism is how this country was founded and how this country is still run!" There is thumping applause; Wright has a cadence and power that make Obama sound like John Kerry. Now the reverend begins to preach. "We are deeply involved in the importing of drugs, the exporting of guns and the training of professional KILLERS.... We believe in white supremacy and black inferiority and believe it more than we believe in God.... We conducted radiation experiments on our own people.... We care nothing about human life if the ends justify the means!" The crowd whoops and amens as Wright builds to his climax. "And. And. And! GAWD! Has GOT! To be SICK! OF THIS SHIT!"

Alarm bells immediately went off at Obama's campaign headquarters, and at the urging of David Axelrod, his chief strategist, Obama called Wright.

"I was at Amherst College, in the office of Paul Sorrentino, the director of religious life there, when Barack called," Wright told me. "Barack said, 'Rev, David [Axelrod] is gonna call you, because we're going to Iowa tomorrow and I don't want you to say anything that will upset the Iowa farmers.' And I said, 'I got it, I got it.' And he said, 'You know, David is a mother hen. He's gonna repeat the same thing to you, but I'm just letting you know what he's gonna call you about.' About an hour later, David called me and said the same thing: 'We're going to Iowa right after the announcement and we don't want to upset the Iowa folks. Is there any way you can work into your invocation something about how egalitarian Barack is, and how he reaches out to people of all ethnic groups.' And I said, 'I got it. I got it.'

"Then, half an hour later, the phone rings again," Wright went on. "It's Barack. And he said, 'Rev, *Rolling Stone*'s gotten ahold of one of your sermons, and they've already given it out to the Hillary people, and it's a big mess. And, you know, you can be over the top at times, and David thinks it's best that you don't do the invocation tomorrow. You're gonna become the media focus and all the attention will be deflected away from my announcing my candidacy. So we're asking that you don't do that. But I have two other requests to make of you.' And I said, 'What are those?' He said, 'Number one, I really want you to be here [in Springfield] and I want you to come and pray privately with Michelle, the kids, and me. Number two, I want my church represented, because my church means a lot to me, so I want Pastor [Otis] Moss [Wright's chosen successor at Trinity United Church of Christ] to do the invocation.' I said, 'Well, okay, let me give you his cell phone number.'

"After Barack hung up, I called Otis and said, 'Man, I just gave your private cell number to Senator Obama, because *Rolling Stone* got ahold of some sermon that they're gonna make a big issue out of, and Barack doesn't want me in front of the public eye. Actually, it's David Axelrod who doesn't want me in front of the cameras. But Barack wants his church to be represented, and he's gonna call you and ask you to come for the invocation.' And Otis said, 'Wait a minute! Eric Whitaker has already called me.'"

Dr. Eric Whitaker, the associate dean and vice president of the University of Chicago Medical Center, was a member of Obama's tight-knit circle of friends. While Whitaker was Illinois health chief, he got caught up in a scandal involving the political fixer Tony Rezko, who was subsequently sent to jail. Whitaker, who was never formally charged with any wrongdoing, traveled with Obama on his campaign plane, played basketball with him, and—unbeknownst to the press corps—secretly handled some of Obama's stickiest personal problems. It was only natural that Obama would turn to Whitaker, a member of Trinity United Church of Christ, to deal with their irascible minister.

"Otis said Eric Whitaker had already called him and tried to persuade him to go to Springfield and deliver the invocation," Wright told me. "Otis was very upset. 'Reverend,' he said, 'I feel I'm being used. They're trying to drive a wedge between us and I'm not gonna do that unless you give me a direct order. I'm not going down to Springfield. You've been his pastor. I just got here.

He doesn't even know me. I'm not gonna do that.'" (In the end, Otis Moss relented and delivered the invocation.)

In the week that followed, Father Michael Pfleger, the bomb-throwing pastor of Saint Sabina's Roman Catholic Church on Chicago's South Side, came to Wright's defense and publicly attacked Eric Whitaker from the pulpit of Trinity United Church of Christ.*

Obama called Wright to complain. "Do you know what it's like being attacked by my own church?" he told Wright and his daughter, Jeri, who was also on the phone.

"Why are your people disrespecting my Daddy who's the pastor of that church?" Jeri Wright shot back. "You called Daddy and asked him would it be all right if Otis gave the invocation, but Eric Whitaker had already made the invitation."

"I didn't know that," Obama said.

"Well, you need to talk to Eric," Jeri said.

David Remnick captured the bitter atmosphere created by this blowup in his book *The Bridge: The Life and Rise of Barack*

---

* Until their falling out, Father Pfleger had been extremely close to Obama, and had encouraged Obama's belief in his God-given destiny. "When Barack was thinking of running for president," Pfleger told me in an interview for this book, "I said to him: 'If you really believe that God is calling you to do this, forget all the norms. But don't forget that the only way this can happen is through God. If you believe God is calling you, do it. But don't forget, if you get it, don't forget it was God first, not people, who got you there.' And Barack said to me, 'Yes, Father, I really believe that my plan in life is to go and become president, and that God has called me to go now.'"

Obama. "And so… poisonous seeds had been planted," Remnick wrote. "[T]he *Rolling Stone* article, one would have guessed, would surely inspire a footrace among media outlets and opposition researchers to comb through all of Wright's sermons of the past thirty-five years…. "

David Remnick's guess turned out to be wrong: media outlets did not engage in a race to follow up on the explosive Jeremiah Wright story. For more than a year, the media ignored the story. Liberal journalists didn't want to rock the boat or do anything to stand in the way of Barack Obama's becoming America's first black president. One could only imagine how these journalists would have behaved if the shoe had been on the other foot and the liberals' bugaboo, President George W. Bush, had sat for twenty years in a white-supremacist church and listened to anti-black rants.

"Never in my memory were so many journalists so intent on effecting [liberal] change as they were during the campaign of 2008," wrote Bernard Goldberg in his bestselling book, *A Slobbering Love Affair: The True (and Pathetic) Story of the Torrid Romance between Barack Obama and the Mainstream Media.* "Sure," Goldberg continued,

> mainstream journalists always root for the Democrat. But this time it was different. This time journalists were not satisfied merely being partisan witnesses to history.

This time they wanted to be real players and determine the outcome. This time they were on a mission—a noble, historic mission, as far as they were concerned. In fact, I could not remember a time when so many supposedly objective reporters had acted so blatantly as full-fledged advocates for one side—and without even a hint of embarrassment.

Then, on March 13, 2008, during the height of the primary battle between Obama and Hillary Clinton, Brian Ross, the chief investigative correspondent of ABC News, broke the media's gentlemen's agreement and broadcast videotapes of Wright's sermons.

"I was surprised that no one else had picked up on the Jeremiah Wright story and pursued the videotapes," Ross said in an interview for this book. "I assumed that the Clinton people would have been after the tapes. But they weren't; they were pushing the Tony Rezko scandal with the media. And not everybody at ABC News was thrilled that I ran with the story. People who liked Obama were not happy with me. In fact, my story ran on *Good Morning America* but was never picked up by *World News Tonight*."

In one particularly damaging sermon broadcast by ABC, Wright fulminated against the treatment of African-Americans: "The government gives them the drugs, builds bigger prisons, passes the three-strike law, and then wants us to sing 'God Bless America.' No! *No!* NO! Not God bless America—God*damn* America!" In another sermon, which Wright delivered on the Sunday after the September 11 terrorist attacks, he charged that al Qaeda's assaults were the result of America's imperialist foreign policy. "We bombed Hiroshima! We bombed Nagasaki! And we nuked far more than the thousands in New York and the Pentagon, and we never batted an eye. We have supported state terrorism against the Palestinians and black South Africans and now we are *indignant* because the stuff we have done overseas is now brought right back into our own front yards! America's *chickens*... are coming *home*... to *roost*."

"Man, the media ate me alive," Wright told me when we met in his office at the Kwame Nkrumah Academy. "After the media went ballistic on me, I received an email offering me money not to preach at all until the November presidential election."

"Who sent the email?" I asked Wright.

"It was from one of Barack's closest friends."

"Who?"

He named him.

"He offered you money?"

"Not directly," Wright said. "He sent the offer to one of the members of the church, who sent it to me."

"How much money did he offer you?"

"One hundred and fifty thousand dollars," Wright said.

"What did Obama do?"

"He sent me a text wishing me happy Easter, which fell that year on March 23—ten days after the ABC News broadcast. And he sent Joshua Dubois, the director of his religious outreach program, to see me. And when Dubois came to Chicago, he didn't know Adam's house cat from Ockham's razor. He spent all day with me trying to figure out what we were going to do next."

"Did Obama himself ever make an effort to see you?"

"Yes," Wright said. "Barack said he wanted to meet me in secret, in a secure place. And I said, 'You're used to coming to my home, you've been here countless times, so what's wrong with coming to my home?' So we met in the living room of the parsonage of Trinity United Church of Christ, at South Pleasant Avenue, right off 95th Street, just Barack and me. I don't know if he had a wire on him. His security was outside somewhere. And one of the first things Barack said was, 'I really wish you wouldn't do any more public speaking until after the November election.' He knew I had some speaking engagements lined up, and he said, 'I wish you wouldn't speak at the NAACP Freedom Fund Dinner and not do the National Press Club appearance. It's gonna hurt the campaign if you do that.'"

"And what did you say?" I asked.

"I said, 'I don't see it that way. And anyway, how am I supposed to support my family? I have a daughter and granddaughter in college, whose tuitions I pay. I've got to earn money.' And he said, 'Well, I wish you wouldn't speak in public. The press is gonna eat you alive.'"

"How did you two leave each other that day in your living room?" I asked.

"Barack said, 'I'm sorry you don't see it the way I do. Do you know what your problem is?' And I said, 'No, what's my problem?' And he said, 'You have to tell the truth.' I said, 'That's a good problem to have. That's a good problem for all preachers to have. That's why I could never be a politician.' And he said, 'It's going to get worse if you go out there and speak. It's really going to get worse.'

"And he was so right."

PART II

AMATEUR HOUR AT THE WHITE HOUSE

"If I win [the presidency], what advice can you guys give me" ... Obama queried. [Former White House chief of staff] Erskine Bowles cut right to the chase. "Leave your friends at home," he said. "They just create problems when you get to Washington." [Valerie] Jarrett and [David] Axelrod looked on, dumbfounded.

—Ron Suskind, *Confidence Men*

CHAPTER 6

DRINKING THE OBAMA KOOL-AID

That fellow seems to me to possess but one idea, and that is a wrong one.

—Samuel Johnson, Boswell's *Life of Johnson*

On the evening of Tuesday, June 30, 2009, Barack Obama invited nine like-minded liberal historians to have dinner with him in the Family Quarters of the White House. His chief of staff, Rahm Emanuel, personally delivered the invitations to each historian with a word of caution: the dinner was to remain private and off the record.

All nine eagerly accepted the invitation, and at the appointed hour they gathered for drinks and hors d'oeuvres in a room decorated with African art, which Barack and Michelle Obama had brought with them to the White House from their home in the Hyde Park section of Chicago. After a while, an usher announced that dinner was being served, and the president led the historians into the dining room, where they hunted for their place cards around a long oval table. The president sat in the middle on one side of the table. Two of his aides—Rahm Emanuel and Valerie Jarrett, the president's powerful behind-the-scenes senior adviser—had been invited to attend, rounding out the number of diners to twelve.

At the time of this dinner, Barack Obama was still enjoying a honeymoon period with the American people. According to the most recent Gallup Poll, 63 percent of Americans approved of the job he was doing. Not surprisingly, he was in an expansive mood as he tucked into his lamb chops and went around the table questioning each historian by name—Doris Kearns Goodwin, Michael Beschloss, Robert Caro, Robert Dallek, David Brinkley, H. W. Brands, David Kennedy, Kenneth Mack, and Gary Wills.

During the presidential campaign, most of the evening's dinner guests had dropped any pretense at historical objectivity. Upon first meeting candidate Obama, Doris Kearns Goodwin (the author of *Team of Rivals: The Political Genius of Abraham Lincoln*) felt she was "in the presence of someone with a really spacious intellect." And Michael Beschloss (*Presidential Courage: Brave Leaders and How They Changed America, 1789–1989*) described Obama as "probably the smartest guy ever to become president," which appeared to put Thomas Jefferson in his place. Like their liberal counterparts in academia, the media, the mainstream churches, and the entertainment industry, the historians had drunk deeply of the Obama Kool-Aid.

Judging from Obama's questions, one subject was foremost in his mind: how he could become a "transformational" president and change the historic trajectory of America's domestic and foreign policy. Despite his woeful lack of experience, he believed he could pull off this formidable feat. In fact, shortly after he won the presidential election, but before he took office, he had confided to David Axelrod, his chief political strategist: "The weird thing is, I know I can do this job. I like dealing with complicated issues. I'm happy to make decisions. I'm looking forward to it. I think it's going to be an easier adjustment for me than the campaign. *Much* easier."

Tonight, in front of nine prominent American historians, Obama wasn't shy about flaunting his famous self-confidence. He intended to bring the Israelis and Palestinians to the negotiating table and create a permanent peace in the Middle East. He would open a constructive dialogue with America's enemies in Iran and North Korea and, through his powers of persuasion, help them see the error of their ways. He'd pass legislation in Washington to revolutionize the country's healthcare system and energy policy. And he'd inject the regulatory hand of the federal government into the American economy in an effort to create "a more just and equitable society."

When several of the historians brought up the difficulties that Lyndon Johnson had faced trying to wage a foreign war while implementing an ambitious domestic agenda, Obama grew testy. He knew better. He could prevail by the force of his personality. He could solve the worst financial crisis since the Great Depression, put millions of people back to work, redistribute wealth, withdraw from Iraq, and reconcile the United States to a less dominant role in the world.

————

It was, by any measure, a breathtaking display of narcissistic grandiosity from a man whose entire political curriculum vitae consisted of seven undistinguished years in the Illinois Senate, two mostly absent years in the United States Senate, and five months and ten days in the White House. Unintentionally, Obama revealed the characteristics that made him totally *unsuited* for the presidency and that would doom him to failure: his extreme haughtiness and excessive pride; his ideological bent as a far-left corporatist; and his astounding amateurism.

These characteristics had already set the pattern of his presidency. He conducted his own foreign policy more than any previous president, including Richard Nixon. He made all the decisions, because he believed that only he understood the issues. He spent his evenings writing decision papers on foreign affairs when, instead, he should have delegated that chore to experts and devoted his time to befriending members of Congress in order to get his bills passed. He still loved making speeches to large, adoring crowds, but he complained to foreign leaders on the QT that he had to waste precious hours talking with "congressmen from Palookaville."

In meetings with his Cabinet and national security team, he acted as though he was the smartest person in the room, which didn't encourage people to speak their minds. He rarely bothered to pick up the phone and seek the advice of outside experts, and he never called the people who had brought him to the dance—those who backed his presidential bid with their money, time, and organizational skills. The Kennedys didn't hear from him. Oprah Winfrey didn't hear from him. Wealthy Jewish donors in Chicago, who had helped fund his 2008 campaign, didn't hear from him. The "First-Day People"—African-American leaders in Chicago who had paved the way for his political ascent—never heard from him, either.

The senior people in his administration proved to be just as inexperienced and inept as Obama when it came to the business of running the government. Members of his inner circle—David Axelrod, campaign manager David Plouffe, press secretary Robert Gibbs, and éminence grise Valerie Jarrett—had proven their mettle in the dark arts of political campaigning, but they had no serious experience in dealing with public policy issues. If they could be said to have any policy exposure at all, it was their ideological enthusiasms for the Left.

What's more, the members of Obama's inner circle didn't treat him as the most important *politician* in America, which he was by virtue of occupying the Oval Office. After all, *politician* was a dirty word in ObamaWorld. Instead, they treated Obama as though he was a movie star or the heavyweight champion of the world, a political Muhammad Ali who never tired of hearing that he was the greatest. "He is the living, breathing apotheosis of the American melting pot," enthused David Axelrod, who privately coined a nickname for his boss: "Black Jesus."

The one discordant note in this chorus of hosannas came from Obama's hard-as-nails chief of staff, Rahm Emanuel, a professional pol who in years to come would privately confess, "I whipped ass up and down, front room and back room, and I got sick and tired of the White House. I got sick of fighting and losing in the White House, and I was eager to leave."

Over the two-hour dinner, Obama and the historians discussed several past presidents. It wasn't clear from Obama's responses which of those presidents he identified with. At one point, Obama seemed to channel the charismatic John F. Kennedy. At another moment, he extolled the virtues of the "transformative" Ronald Reagan. Then again, it was the saintly Lincoln... or the New Deal's "Happy Warrior," Franklin Roosevelt... or...

In the words of Victor Davis Hanson, who, like other *conservative* historians, had not been invited to attend the dinner, the new president seemed to be looking for "a presidential identity not his own.... endlessly trying on new presidential masks."

Obama told the historians at the table that he had come up with a slogan for his administration. "I'm thinking of calling it 'A New Foundation,'" he said.

Doris Kearns Goodwin suggested that "A New Foundation" might not be the wisest choice for a motto.

"Why not?" the president asked.

"It sounds," said Goodwin, "like a woman's girdle."

If the meeting proved anything, it was that Barack Obama didn't have the faintest idea 1) *who* he was; 2) *why* he had been elected president; and 3) *how* to be the commander in chief and chief executive of the United States of America.

In short, he didn't know what he didn't know.

He believed, wrongly, that his so-called "personal narrative" had gotten him elected. Even as president, he never tired of telling the same old stories—more myth than reality—about his idealistic white mother and brilliant African father; his American-as-apple-pie white grandparents, Gramps and Toot; his cockeyed Indonesian stepfather Lolo Soetoro; and his transformation from a confused young man of mixed race named Barry to a proud African-American adult named Barack Hussein Obama.

He further believed, wrongly, that he was not only a different kind of leader by virtue of his race, strange name, and exotic upbringing, but that he was a child of destiny, a special person who had been singled out for great things. In his mind, he had been elected to be a transformational president and to save America from itself.

None of this was true. Barack Obama wasn't elected because of his charisma and biography. And he certainly wasn't elected to turn America into a European-style quasi-socialist country in which the state controls economic and social matters. The political stars had aligned for him in the election year of 2008 because the American people were scared to death about the economy, fed up with George W. Bush and the spendthrift Republicans, disillusioned by the seemingly endless war in Iraq, and sick at heart over the decline of their society's values.

But Obama couldn't see any of that.

He was blind to reality because he suffered from what could only be described as a messianic complex—meaning that he believed he was destined to become America's savior. "My attitude is that you don't want to just be the president," Obama told an interviewer for *Men's Vogue*. "You want to change the country."

For a long time, people didn't understand that there was a method in his madness. As Shelby Steele, a senior fellow at Stanford University's Hoover Institution, pointed out, "Among today's liberal elite, bad faith in America is a sophistication, a kind of hipness. More importantly, it is the perfect formula for political and government power. It rationalizes power in the name of intervening against evil—I will use the government to intervene against the evil tendencies of American life (economic inequality, structural racism and sexism, corporate greed, neglect of the environment and so on)...."

Obama's acolytes in academia, the media, the churches, and the world of entertainment encouraged this dangerous delusion. Micah Tillman, a lecturer in philosophy at the Catholic University of America, said: "Barack Obama is the Platonic philosopher king we've been looking for for the past 2,400 years." At a campaign rally in South Carolina, Oprah Winfrey had referred to Obama as "The One," a reference to both Jesus Christ and Neo from the movie *The Matrix*. The *New York Times* called his election "a national catharsis." His hometown newspaper, the *Chicago Sun-Times*, wrote, "The first African-American president of the

Harvard Law Review has a movie-star smile and more than a little mystique. Also, we just like to say his name. We are considering taking it as a mantra."

Obama's political apostles never seemed to tire of coming up with fresh examples of his divinity. Some examples:

MSNBC's Chris Matthews: "I've been following politics since I was about 5. I've never seen anything like this. This is bigger than Kennedy. [Obama] comes along, and he seems to have the answers. This is the New Testament."

Newsweek **editor Evan Thomas:** "In a way Obama is standing above the country, above the world. He's sort of God. He's going to bring all the different sides together."

Film director Spike Lee: "You'll have to measure time by 'Before Obama' and 'After Obama'.... Everything's going to be affected by this seismic change in the universe."

Jonathan Alter in his book, *The Promise: President Obama, Year One*:

> Rabbi David Saperstein, reading from Psalms in English and Hebrew, noticed from the altar that the good men and women of the congregation that day, including the Bidens and other dignitaries, had not yet stood. Finally Bishop Vashti McKenzie of the African Methodist Church asked that everyone rise. At that moment Saperstein saw something from his angle of vision:

"If I had seen it in a movie I would have groaned and said, 'Give me a break. That's so trite.'" A beam of morning light shown [sic] through the stained-glass windows and illuminated the president-elect's face. Several of the clergy and choir on the altar who also saw it marveled afterward about the presence of the Divine.

The absurd, not to say blasphemous comparison of Obama to the Almighty became so embarrassing that Vice President Joe Biden couldn't resist the opportunity to tease the president about his messiah complex. Speaking at the 2009 white-tie Gridiron Club Dinner, Biden said. "[President Obama] can't be here tonight because he's busy getting ready for Easter. He thinks it's about him."

During his dinner with the historians, Obama indicated that he had a preference for a corporatist political system in which the economy would be collectively managed by big employers, big unions, and government officials through a formal mechanism at the national level. Also known as state capitalism, it is a system in which the government picks winners and promotes economic growth.

This corporatist approach was hardly a new idea. It had been around for more than one hundred and fifty years. It had been tried in the 1930s and 1940s by Benito Mussolini's Italian Fascists, and in Europe after World War II by democratic-socialist governments in Greece, Italy, Spain, and Portugal, among others. In America during the 1970s and 1980s, leftwing Democratic presidential candidates Gary Hart and Michael Dukakis revived the idea, arguing that America should replace free-market capitalism with what they called "a neo-corporatist state."

Though the corporatist idea had an unbroken record of failure both in Europe and America, where voters had decisively rejected Gary Hart and Michael Dukakis, Obama was determined to embrace this discredited economic, political, and social philosophy. He planned to achieve his "transformational" presidency by vastly expanding the reach of Washington into the everyday life of American citizens.

In that regard, the American president whom Obama most closely resembled was not JFK, Reagan, Lincoln, or Franklin Roosevelt. It was Woodrow Wilson, whose conception of himself was aptly described by the noted conservative historian Forrest McDonald (also missing at the White House dinner) as "little short of messianic." Indeed, McDonald wrote about Wilson:

> … the day after his election, the Democratic national chairman called on him to confer about appointments, only to be rebuffed by Wilson's statement, "Before we proceed, I wish it clearly understood that I owe you nothing. Remember that God ordained that I should be the next President of the United States." He was a master of oratory who described every issue, no matter how trivial, in terms of a great moral crusade, always with himself as the nation's (and later the world's)

moral leader—and he believed what he was saying. Given this attitude, it followed that people who opposed him were unenlightened or evil; it was therefore impossible to meet them halfway.

Forrest McDonald's description of Woodrow Wilson captures Barack Obama to a T.

―――――――

In the fall of 2011—shortly after Obama botched the budget-deficit negotiations with Congress, and the United States government lost its Triple-A credit rating for the first time in history—I met under hush-hush conditions with one of the historians who had dined at the White House with Obama during the infancy of his presidency. We met in a restaurant on the outskirts of a large American city, where we were unlikely to be seen. Our conversation, which lasted for nearly two hours, was conducted under the condition of anonymity.

I wanted to know how this historian, who had once drunk the Obama Kool-Aid, matched the president's promise with his performance. By this time, most of Obama's supporters were puzzled by a sense of disconnect between the strictly-on-message presidential candidate and the president who was adrift and elusive. The satirical TV show *The Onion News Network* broadcast a faux story that the real Barack Obama had been kidnapped just hours after the election and replaced by an imposter.

Disillusioned liberals viewed Obama as a failed messiah. But conservatives had never fallen for the messianic talk. To conservatives, Obama's problems stemmed less from his inflated self-image than from his unmitigated incompetence. He was the community organizer who had never held a real job and had brought the country to the brink of ruin because of his callow understanding of the way the world worked.

I wondered if the historian I met at the deli agreed with this assessment.

"There's no doubt that Obama has turned out to be a major enigma and disappointment," the historian admitted. "He waged such a brilliant campaign, first against Hillary Clinton in the primaries, then against John McCain in the general election. For a long time, I found it hard to understand why he couldn't translate his political savvy into effective governance.

"But I think I know the answer now," the historian continued. "Since the beginning of his administration, Obama hasn't been able to capture the public's imagination and inspire people to follow him. Vision isn't enough in a president. Great presidents not only have to enunciate their vision; they must lead by example and inspiration. Franklin Roosevelt spoke to the individual. He and Ronald Reagan had the ability to make each American feel that the president cared deeply and personally about them.

"That quality has been lacking in Obama. People don't feel that he's on their side. The irony is that he was supposed to be such a brilliant orator, but in fact he's turned out to be a failure as a communicator. And his failure to connect with people has had nothing to do with the choice of his words or how well he delivers his speeches. It's something much more fundamental than that.

"The American people have come to realize that, in Barack Obama, they elected a man as president who does not know how to lead. He lacks an executive sense. He doesn't know how to run things. He's not a manager. He hasn't been able to bring together the best and brightest talents. Not to put too fine a point on it, he's in over his head."

CHAPTER 7

BUNGLER-IN-CHIEF

[Obama's Nobel Peace Prize] would be like
giving someone an Oscar in the hope that it would
encourage them to make a decent motion picture.

—Christopher Hitchens

Calling Barack Obama an amateur can be tricky business. After all, amateurs are often viewed in a positive light. In fiction, Agatha Christie's Miss Marple is an amateur detective, and the foppish young English nobleman Sir Percy Blackeney turns out to be the dashing Scarlet Pimpernel. In real life, two of history's greatest scientists, Charles Darwin and Gregor Mendel, were amateurs. So was the great golfer Bobby Jones. And who can forget the finest amateur boxer of all time, Cassius Clay, who won the light-heavyweight gold medal at the 1960 Summer Olympics before he turned professional as Muhammad Ali?

Obama would appear to be the polar opposite of the amateur who does what he does for the pure pleasure of it. No matter how much Obama likes to parade as a nonpartisan reformer, he is, in fact, the product of Chicago-style politics, which is a byword for patronage, nepotism, bribery, and corruption.

Since 1972, four Illinois governors (out of seven) have been convicted of corruption. "A new report... documents the extent to which the state of Illinois and the city of Chicago have been hotbeds of corruption," reports the February 25, 2012, issue of *The Economist*.

> Chicago... has the dubious distinction of being the federal district with the most convictions since 1976. Since then, 1,828 elected officials, appointees, government employees and a few private individuals have been convicted of corruption in Illinois, and 84 percent of these were in its Northern District—a judicial zone which contains the entire Chicago metropolitan area. During this time around one-third of the city's aldermen have been convicted of corruption. No mayors have been convicted or indicted—not even Bill Thompson, who was backed by Al Capone.

Chicago is where Obama cut his political teeth. His wife Michelle worked for Mayor Daley's political machine, as did his senior adviser, Valerie Jarrett. Obama and his crew of Chicago operatives don't abide by the Marquess of Queensberry Rules of political combat. As Sean Connery memorably said of "the Chicago way" in the movie *The Untouchables*: "He brings a knife to the fight, you bring a gun; he puts one of yours in the hospital, you put one of his in the morgue."

"If we have learned anything about Barack Obama the past three years it's that he enjoys hitting," columnist Daniel Henninger wrote in the *Wall Street Journal*. "He will be merciless with [the Republican nominee]. Ask Hillary. Ask the respectful Republicans that Obama [has] pistol-whipped.... Ask Wall Street's Democrats."

So what do I mean when I call such a bare-knuckled political warrior an amateur? I simply mean this: judged by the skillset that is necessary for the chief executive and commander in chief of the United States of America, Obama is the Bungler-in-Chief.

"Obama has a political sense, but he lacks an executive sense," says Walter Anderson, a leadership expert whose lectures at the New School for Social Research in New York City were turned into a bestselling book, *The Confidence Course*. "He has the same vulnerability that many legislators have; he's skillful at getting elected, but he's often lost when it comes to governing and inspiring others. In my view, it's a mistake to compare Obama to Jimmy Carter, as some do. Carter was a micromanager in all things. Obama is anything but."

"Obama is politically astute," says Tavis Smiley, the African-American talk-show host who has often criticized Obama. "I was in awe of how well run and on message his presidential campaign was. In all my life, I never saw a campaign run so brilliantly. And so it's been interesting to see how off course and off track Obama has gotten in the White House. And what's occurred to me is that campaigning and governing are entirely different things, and that all the things that served Obama so well in the campaign have come back to haunt him in his governance."

William Safire, the late *New York Times* columnist and lexicographer, might have had Barack Obama in mind when he noted in *Safire's Political Dictionary*:

> Because there are a great many more amateurs than pros, the public image of the amateur is that of a fresh-faced, civic-minded citizen out to do battle for a cause he believes in, versus the cigar-chomping image of the political professional.... The appearance of being an amateur, then, is something to be coveted; the act of doing political work amateurishly is something to be avoided.

Obama has cultivated the *appearance* of being a political amateur. He likes to be seen as above the fray. He hates to be seen getting his hands dirty in the nitty-gritty of politics. During his presidency, he has rarely appeared at the Democratic Party's most important annual event—the Jefferson Jackson Day fundraising dinner. He lets others in the White House deconstruct polling data and analyze electoral maps, because he thinks that such behavior is beneath him. And he refuses to make "robo-calls," recorded phone messages asking people to go out and vote.

"Obama does little to disguise his disdain for Washington and the conventions of modern politics," writes the *New York Times'*

Peter Baker, the author of a book on the impeachment of Bill Clinton. "When he emerges from the Oval Office during the day, aides say, he sometimes pauses before the split-screen television in the outer reception area, soaks in the cable chatter, then shakes his head and walks away. 'He's still never gotten comfortable here,' a top White House official told me. He has little patience for what Valerie Jarrett, a senior adviser, calls 'the inevitable theatrics of Washington.'... He has yet to fully decide whether he is of Washington or apart from it."

Obama's consigliere, Valerie Jarrett, is even blunter about it. She told *New Yorker* editor David Remnick that Obama was "just too talented to do what ordinary people do."

All of this helps explain why Obama bungled last year's deliberations by the Joint Select Committee on Deficit Reduction, otherwise known as the Supercommittee. "A Ronald Reagan or a Bill Clinton would have been much more effectively engaged in twisting arms and, where necessary, dispensing favors," wrote *The Economist*. Obama's detachment from the political battle, the British magazine went on to say, "should not have been surprising, given his lamentable failure a year ago to endorse the effective and brave conclusions of the Bowles-Simpson deficit commission that he personally appointed."

Obama's arrogance, his sense of superiority, and his air of haughtiness—but above all, his *amateurism*—are responsible for his record of political fiascos. Two days after his inauguration, he overruled his chief of staff, Rahm Emanuel, and signed orders saying that the prison camp at Guantanamo Bay would be closed within a year. At the time of the signing, he didn't have the faintest idea where he would put the terrorists. It turned out that nobody in America wanted terrorists in their backyard, and so nearly four years later most of them are still there in Gitmo.

Again against the advice of Rahm Emanuel, Obama supported Attorney General Eric Holder's harebrained scheme to send Khalid Sheikh Mohammed, the mastermind of the September 11 terrorist attacks, to New York City to stand trial in a civilian court not far from the site of the ruins of the World Trade Center. Ultimately, Obama had to abandon the notion of trying Khalid Sheikh Mohammed as a civilian.

Democratic political strategist James Carville, a native of Louisiana, lambasted Obama for the "political stupidity" of his response to the calamitous oil spill in the Gulf of Mexico. "The president doesn't get down here in the middle of this," Carville said. "... I have no idea of why they [the White House] didn't seize this thing. I have no idea of why their attitude was so hands off here. The president of the United States could've come down here, he could've been involved with the families of these eleven people [who died in the explosion]. He could've demanded a plan in anticipation of this.... It just looks like he's not involved in this. Man, you got to get down here and take control of this."

Obama's view of himself as a superior human being who isn't bound by the same rules as other politicians has frequently gotten him into hot water. While campaigning for the presidency, he refused to wear a flag pin, as though he agreed with Samuel Johnson's supercilious remark that "patriotism is the last refuge of a scoundrel." When his missing flag pin became an issue in the campaign, he started wearing one. After he won the White House, his failure to attend church services resurrected old questions about whether he was a Christian. To tamp down the criticism, he started showing up at church services near the White House, making sure there were photographers on hand to record his pious devotions.

But to a remarkable degree, Obama has compounded his amateurism by failing to learn from his mistakes and correct them. Case in point: When the president campaigned for the 2009 stimulus package at the start of his presidency, he promised that large chunks of the money would go to "shovel-ready projects." Two years after he signed the $800 billion package, a shamefaced Obama acknowledged, "There's no such thing as shovel-ready projects." Yet, though the initial "stimulus" was a flop, that didn't stop Obama from going back to Congress to ask for more money: a budget-busting $450 billion.

Another case in point: In September 2011, Obama decided he wanted to address a joint session of Congress in order to lay out his agenda on job creation. Trouble was, no one in the clueless Obama White House realized that Congress wasn't in session, and that the president's choice of date fell on the same evening as a planned Republican presidential debate. The president was forced to accept another date and time, which turned out to be just as embarrassing, because it conflicted with the regular NFL season opener between the Green Bay Packers and the New Orleans Saints.

Obama's most glaring political error was to make a massive overhaul of the nation's healthcare system his first priority instead of concentrating, as he should have, on the economy and jobs.

"Early on, Emanuel argued for a smaller bill with popular items, such as expanding health coverage for children and young adults, that could win some Republican support," noted *Washington Post* columnist Dana Milbank. "He opposed the public option as a needless distraction. The president disregarded that strategy and sided with Capitol Hill liberals who hoped to ram a larger, less popular bill through Congress with Democratic votes only. The result was, as the world now knows, disastrous."[*]

What's more, even after Obama got his signature healthcare bill passed by Congress, he never found a way to sell it to the American people. It was as if he was more interested in having a signing ceremony than in what he signed.

"To me," said a former staff director of a major Senate committee, "that signals inexperience, because as president Obama has not managed to get any benefit from the major piece of legislation that he's passed. It's almost as though he doesn't want to talk about it. He's not out there touting these things because he's not sure how he really feels about them. From my experience dealing with the White House, I'm not convinced that Obama's wedded to these programs. Leaving aside the campaign rhetoric—give hope a chance and all that stuff—what will Obama bleed for? What will he go to the mat for? What does this guy believe in his core?"

At the beginning of 2012, just as the limping American economy started to show some signs of movement and Obama's poll

---

[*] When Obama overruled Emanuel on healthcare, he told him: "I wasn't sent here to do school uniforms."

ratings began to stir, he stepped in deep doo-doo again. This time, he announced that all religious-affiliated institutions would be required to pay for insurance that covered birth control, including contraception. As could have been predicted, there was an instant backlash from the hierarchy of the Catholic Church as well as from both conservative- and liberal-leaning Catholics. Even Obama's true believers found it hard to comprehend the president's amateurish decision, which stomped on the religious liberty clause of the First Amendment. *Hardball*'s liberal chatterbox, Chris Matthews, called it "frightening," and *Washington Post* columnist E. J. Dionne, an ardent Obama loyalist, wrote that Obama had "utterly botched" the issue.

That Obama could so completely misread the public mood was nothing new. It recalled the time during the 2008 presidential campaign when he criticized white working-class voters in Pennsylvania and the Midwest for clinging to "guns or religion." After Hillary Clinton jumped on him for those comments, saying, "The people of faith I know don't cling to religion because they are materially poor, but because they are spiritually rich," Obama was forced to apologize and eat crow.

And that's exactly what happened with his regulation requiring religious-affiliated institutions to provide birth control insurance. In the midst of the firestorm of criticism, he called a press conference and, looking glum and sounding resentful, announced a policy to quiet his critics. Under the new policy, health insurance companies—not religious employers—would pay for contraceptives.

To many conservatives, it was a distinction without a difference. Obama had only made matters worse. "Insurance companies won't be making donations," editorialized the *Wall Street Journal*. "Drug makers will still charge for the pill. Doctors will still bill for reproductive treatment. The reality, as with all mandated benefits, is that these costs will be borne eventually via higher premiums. The balloon may be squeezed differently over time, and insurers may amortize the cost differently over time, but eventually prices will find an equilibrium. Notre Dame will still pay for birth control, even if it is nominally carried by a third-party corporation."

CHAPTER 8

CLARK KENT

*With all of Obama's rhetorical brilliance
and flash, he went into the phone booth as
Superman and came out as Clark Kent.*

—Presidential historian Fred I. Greenstein

To put all this in perspective, I asked former Secretary of State
James Baker, who served as chief of staff in President Reagan's first administration, how he would rate Obama's performance.

"The conditions under which Barack Obama and Ronald Reagan came to power are startlingly similar," said Baker, who is widely regarded as the most effective chief of staff in modern presidential history. "Both inherited a terrible economic situation. But Reagan set about focusing with laser-like intensity on economic issues. [Then Secretary of State] Al Haig wanted to take some action in the Caribbean while we were trying to focus entirely on the economy, and we shut him down. By contrast, Obama didn't focus on the big problem of the economy. He didn't even draft his own stimulus package; he subcontracted it out to the Democrats in Congress.

"Immediately after the drubbing Obama took in the 2010 midterm elections," Baker continued, "I was asked to come to Washington to meet with him. His secretary called my office to set up a time. Then I got a call from [chief of staff] Bill Daley. 'I understand you're going to meet with the president,' Daley told me. 'Would you stop by and meet with me afterward?' Then I got another call, this one from [national security adviser] Tom Donilon, who said the same thing as Daley. In the Reagan administration, we would never have scheduled a meeting with the president that the chief of staff and the national security adviser found out about later.

"All this comes from the fact that, before he became president, Obama never had the responsibility for running anything. He's a policy wonk; he's very smart, very knowledgeable. But he was a community organizer, and a community organizer doesn't have the lines of authority that you have when you're running an organization."

Obama's handling of the 2009 fiscal crisis showed an alarming lack of experience and a complete ignorance of how Washington works. For instance, during the presidential race, Obama campaigned against earmarks—the notorious legislative gimmick used by congressmen and senators to allocate funds for favorite projects in their home districts. Yet, when House Speaker Nancy

Pelosi and Senate Majority Leader Harry Reid sent an omnibus spending bill with $8 billion worth of earmarks to the White House, Obama naïvely believed Pelosi and Reid, who told him that that was the only way he could get his $800 billion stimulus bill passed. Obama signed the omnibus spending bill with all the earmarks intact, signaling that the barons of Capitol Hill could roll the amateurish president.

For a long time, some people—especially those in the liberal mainstream media—thought that Obama would somehow make up for what he lacked in experience with his oratorical skills. Liberals considered Obama to be a great communicator—right up there with such masters as Franklin Roosevelt, Ronald Reagan, and Bill Clinton.

Not anymore.

Most of his recent speeches have fallen flat. Americans have tuned him out. His 2012 State of the Union address was seen by 37.8 million television viewers—down from the 52.3 million people who tuned in to his first address to Congress in 2009. As Maureen Dowd noted in the *New York Times*: "[Bill] Clinton will often forcefully—and feelingly—frame the argument for Obama policies… in a way that Obama himself, once hailed as a master communicator, can't seem to muster."

———

Other presidents have entered the White House as amateurs. John F. Kennedy immediately comes to mind. JFK stumbled badly during his first year in office; the Bay of Pigs calamity was only the most notable of his many mistakes. But he grew in the job and was well on his way to becoming an effective chief executive when he was cut down by an assassin's bullet in Dallas.

So why hasn't Obama grown in the job?

There are several answers to that question, which we will explore in depth in the pages that follow. But for now, the short answer is:

Barack Obama has the wrong temperament for the presidency.

Supreme Court Justice Oliver Wendell Holmes Jr. famously said about Franklin Roosevelt that he had a "second class mind, but a first class temperament." The opposite is true of Barack Obama, who for all his academic credentials is not cut out by temperament to be the leader of the free world.

By all accounts, Obama was elected to a job for which he has little relish. He doesn't find joy in being president. Like Richard Nixon and Jimmy Carter, he is an introvert who prefers his own company to that of others. *The Times'* Peter Baker puts it this way: Obama is "someone who finds extended contact with groups of people outside his immediate circle to be draining. He can rouse a stadium of 80,000 people, but that audience is an impersonal monolith; smaller group settings can be harder for him.... While [Bill] Clinton made late-night phone calls around Washington to vent or seek advice, Obama rarely reaches outside the tight groups of advisers."

"I've been in a lot of meetings with him on foreign policy," a former State Department official told me. "While I was in the room, he'd get phone calls from heads of state, and more than once I heard him say, 'I can't believe I've got to meet with all these congressmen from Podunk city to get my bills passed.' And when the meeting with him was over, it was over—no lingering, no schmoozing on the way out. There was no clinging to personal relationship like with Bill Clinton."

In his study of the presidency, *Hail to the Chief,* historian Robert Dallek lists five qualities that have been constants in the men who have most effectively fulfilled the oath of office: 1) vision; 2) political pragmatism; 3) national consensus; 4) personal connection with the people; and 5) credibility.

Dallek places the greatest emphasis on numbers 4 and 5. "The best of our presidents," he writes, "have always recognized that leadership required a personal connection between the president and the people, or that the power of the Oval Office rests to a great degree on the affection of the country for its chief. From Washington to Lincoln to the two Roosevelts and, most recently, Reagan, the force of presidential personality has been a major factor in determining a president's fate.... [P]residents who are unable to earn the trust of their countrymen are governors who cannot govern and lead."

Barack Obama has been unable to earn the trust of his countrymen because he is, at heart, predominantly concerned with his own thoughts and ideas and feelings rather than the thoughts and ideas and feelings of the people he was elected to serve. He believes that he was chosen as president to save a wayward America from its dependency on free-market capitalism. This has led him to push clumsy and unpopular far-left policies—universal healthcare, Wall Street bailouts, cap and trade, green jobs, and renewable energy—at the expense of rational policies aimed at putting America back to work.

CHAPTER 9

GROUND ZERO

She knows the buttons, the soft spots,
the history, the context.

—Michelle Obama, speaking about Valerie Jarrett

"If it wasn't for Valerie Jarrett, there'd be no Barack Obama to complain about."

The speaker was a member of the White House press corps who has covered the Obamas, husband and wife, since their early days on the political scene. My colleague and I were sitting in a Mexican restaurant in Washington, eating chimichangas and exchanging notes about Valerie Jarrett, or VJ as she is known in the West Wing.

Jarrett is ground zero in the Obama operation, the first couple's first friend and consigliere. Once asked by a reporter if he

ran *every* decision by Jarrett, Obama answered without hesita-
tion: "Yep. Absolutely." Her official title is a mouthful—senior
adviser and assistant to the president for intergovernmental
affairs and public engagement—but it doesn't begin to do justice
to her unrivaled status in the White House. Nor does it explain
her responsibility, which has gone largely unnoticed by the
public, for the incompetence and amateurism that have been the
hallmark of Obama's time in office.

Jarrett occupies a piece of prime real estate in the White
House—Karl Rove and Hillary Clinton's old office on the second
floor of the West Wing. She has an all-access pass to meetings she
chooses to attend: one day she'll show up at a National Security
Council meeting; the next day, she'll sit in on a briefing on the
federal budget. When Oval Office meetings break up, Jarrett is
often the one who stays behind to talk privately with the president.

At 6:30 on many evenings, Jarrett can be seen slipping upstairs
to the Family Quarters, where she dines with the Obamas and
their two daughters, Sasha and Malia. She is the only member of
the White House staff who goes on vacations with the Obamas.
She is also one of the few people in Washington besides Michelle
Obama and Barack's live-in mother-in-law, Marian Robinson,
who is on such familiar terms with the president that she can call
him by his first name to his face.

"Valerie is the quintessential insider," one of her longtime
friends told me. "She functions as the eyes, ears, and nose of the
president and first lady. She tells them who's saying what about
who, who's loyal and who's not. She advises them about who
they should see when they visit a city or a foreign country.

She determines who gets invited to the White House and who is left out in the cold."

Jarrett is supposed to be the point person for the administration's efforts to keep in touch with the outside world—everyone from senators to foreign dignitaries. Obama sent her to talk to the Dalai Lama before he visited China. However, if you talk to Democratic donors, businessmen, congressmen, and African-Americans, as I have, it turns out that Jarrett is far better at giving people the cold shoulder than at welcoming them with open arms. Like Obama, she has a fundamental lack of respect for businessmen. In a typical blunder that sent shudders through the business community, she dismissed Tom Donohue, the highly regarded CEO of the U.S. Chamber of Commerce, as irrelevant, saying that she preferred to deal with "real" industry executives.

"I have always thought Valerie was a liability," a prominent donor told the *Washington Post*. "I've talked to people in the White House about it, and they have agreed with me, but they are scared to say anything."

Behind its "no-drama" façade, the Obama administration has been rocked by major personnel shakeups (both the president and the first lady have gone through several chiefs of staff), but Jarrett is still the indispensable person in the mix. When speculation arose that Jarrett might want the Senate seat vacated by Obama when he became president, Michelle put the kibosh on the idea.

"I told her," said Michelle, "that I wanted her [in the White House], in that position, that it would give me a sense of comfort to know that [my husband] had somebody like her there by his side."

The president has made it abundantly clear that he feels the same way. As he told the *New York Times*: "Valerie is one of my oldest friends. Over time, I think our relationship evolved to the point where she's like a sibling to me... I trust her completely."

―――――――

Trying to figure out Valerie Jarrett's mysterious hold on the president and first lady is a favorite guessing game in the parlors and dining rooms of Washington.

In part, her influence stems from the fact that Jarrett is the president's trusted watchdog. She protects the vainglorious and thin-skinned Obama from critics and complainers who might deflate his ego. No one gets past Jarrett and sees the president if they have a grievance, or a chip on their shoulder, or even an incompatible point of view. That goes for such high-profile supporters as Oprah Winfrey and Caroline Kennedy, who have been largely frozen out of the White House because Jarrett believes they would use the opportunity of a meeting with Obama to push their own competing political agendas.

In part, too, Obama views Jarrett as the voice of authentic blackness in a White House that is staffed largely by whites. Jarrett comes from the top rung of African-American society, and Obama—a man who struggled for years with questions about his black identity and status—has always been more than a little in awe of Jarrett's pedigree.

No minority group is more conscious of social status than blacks. While whites often see the black population in the United

States as monolithic, Pulitzer Prize-winning columnist Eugene Robinson, in his book *Disintegration: The Splintering of Black America*, sees not one, but essentially five distinct Black Americas: a mainstream middle class; a large, abandoned minority living in poverty and dysfunction; a small "Transcendent" elite with enormous power and wealth; individuals of mixed race; and communities of recent black immigrants.

Jarrett comes from the class of light-skinned "Transcendent" elites. "Among African-Americans, there is a keen perception of the gradation of skin color," says Rahni Flowers, who was Michelle Obama's hairdresser from the time she was eighteen years old until she went to Washington. "It often determines how successful you are and what opportunities you are given. Michelle is darker; she's not from the class of so-called 'high-yellow' blacks. Many African-American women are proud of the fact that she is a typical-looking black woman in hue and hair."

Whereas Barack and Michelle Obama came from modest middle-class backgrounds, Jarrett sprang from one of America's most distinguished black families. The Robert Taylor Homes— the largest housing development project in America when it was completed in 1962—was named after her grandfather, a noted African-American activist. Her father, James Bowman, was a famous pathologist and geneticist, who was a member of Sigma Pi Phi, a national fraternity of high-achieving blacks that was founded in 1904. Her mother, Barbara Taylor Bowman, was a psychologist who helped found the Erikson Institute for child development in Chicago. Valerie attended Stanford University and the University of Michigan Law School, and was married for a time to the late Dr. Robert Jarrett, the son of famed *Chicago Sun-Times* columnist Vernon Jarrett, who was responsible for landing Valerie her first city job, as Mayor Richard M. Daley's corporation counsel.

For all their Ivy League degrees, Barack and Michelle Obama were originally social outsiders in Chicago, which boasts more black millionaires than any other city in America. The Obamas didn't break into the exclusive world of Chicago politics and money until Jarrett met Michelle and hired her to work for Mayor Daley. At the time, Jarrett was Daley's deputy chief of staff, and was known in Chicago as the "public black face" of the Daley administration.

"She talked the liberal talk, but she didn't walk the liberal walk, because she was essentially a creature of the Daley Machine," said a former community organizer who worked with Jarrett.

In addition, Jarrett was a member of the boards of exclusive cultural institutions in Chicago, such as the Symphony Orchestra and the Art Institute. Thanks to her high-level connections in the nexus of politics, culture, and money, she was able to introduce Obama to the affluent African-American and Jewish communities in Chicago.

In the eyes of many African-Americans, however, Jarrett's elitist background helps explain her condescending manner and inability to help Obama where it counts the most—remaining on good terms with his diverse and far-flung constituencies.

"Growing up, Valerie had very limited contact with African-American working-class people," said a Chicagoan who worked with her. "The closest she came to the [mostly black] South Side was when she drove through it in her Mercedes convertible with the top down. She never had to work her way up. Everything was handed to her because of her pedigree. She is naturally attracted to African-Americans who have a pedigree like hers. I question her capability. I never felt that she was astute enough to do her job in the White House."

Despite her impeccable social credentials, Jarrett's record before she went to Washington was spotty at best. After Mayor Daley made her commissioner of planning, she became embroiled in a massive screw-up in the city's public housing revitalization plan, which cost Chicago millions of dollars in overruns. Daley fired her without any explanation.

"I've known Valerie since she became commissioner of planning," said a Chicago real estate developer. "She served her master, she was a functionary of her master, Richie Daley, and I didn't like her. She would be cunning and not straightforward. She was very tough on people. She'd go to the wall for Daley and make sure her boss's wishes were carried out. But her advice to Daley was damaging to other people and to her benefit and standing with the mayor. Her job was never policy, and she's never been an operational person. She was an implementer. And she made sure that her fingerprints weren't on things."

Later, after Jarrett left city hall, she became the CEO of Habitat Executive Services, where she earned $300,000 in salary and $550,000 in deferred compensation. She managed a federally subsidized housing complex that was seized by the government after inspectors found crime-infested slum conditions and widespread blight.

Throughout her career, Jarrett has failed upward. Today she is at the pinnacle of power as Michelle Obama's closest confidant and Barack Obama's political soul mate. When I asked the historian Doris Kearns Goodwin if she could think of anyone in the past who occupied such a special relationship with *both* the president and first lady, she mentioned Harry Hopkins, one of Franklin and Eleanor Roosevelt's closest advisers. Other historians, searching their memory, came up with the name of Michael Deaver, who was a member of Ronald Reagan's staff and an intimate friend of Nancy Reagan's.

But unlike Hopkins, who was the chief architect of Roosevelt's New Deal, and Deaver, who had a thirty-year career working for Reagan, Jarrett came to her White House job with few if any achievements. Many insiders in Chicago and Washington find her friendly and pleasant enough, but off the record they use almost identical words to describe her: "She doesn't have the stuff to be a principal adviser to the president of the United States."

"She has no international experience and no background in economics or fiscal policy," said Michael Lavin, the retired vice chairman of the global accounting firm KPMG and a major force in Chicago's social and cultural institutions. "There were people in previous Democratic administrations who were real heavyweights. But Valerie is no [former Secretary of State] Cyrus Vance."

"I was at a dinner where Valerie sat at our table for ten minutes, and I wasn't particularly impressed," said a major Obama donor. "She didn't say anything interesting. I expected her to be smarter. She ain't no Karl Rove. Karl Rove would eat her for breakfast."

CHAPTER 10

VALERIE V. RAHM

The first method for estimating the intelligence of
a ruler is to look at the men he has around him.

—Niccolò Machiavelli

Not long after Rahm Emanuel returned to Chicago to run for mayor of the Windy City, a hard-bitten old pol buttonholed him on a street where he was campaigning. "You're nobody's fool," the old pol said, "so why did the White House reek of rank amateurism on your watch?"

"I fucked up," Emanuel replied.

"Bullshit!" the pol said. "I don't accept that excuse."

"Why not?" Emanuel asked, taken aback.

"Because nobody ever heard from the president while you were there, and yet you and I know that every politician's got a list on his desk of people to call," said the old pol. "Every politician has such a list. Maybe two, three, four hundred calls come into the president every day and he can answer only four or five or six. You need someone who knows how to make that list, the call list. You tell me Obama didn't have a list? I don't believe it. He had a list when he was raising money to run for the White House. You tell me that that list didn't exist anymore?"

Emanuel tried to get a word in edgewise, but the pol had worked himself into a lather and was in no mood to listen.

"For chrisssake, it was never your list anyway, Rahm," he said. "During the primary campaign, you were working with the Hillary people. The Obama people had their own list. Why didn't Obama call people on that fucking list?"

Emanuel thought for a moment, then said: "I guess it all comes down to one person."

"Who's that?"

"Valerie Jarrett."

By general consensus, Valerie Jarrett, the White House official responsible for "public engagement," has conspicuously failed to engage. I heard this complaint about Jarrett from practically everyone I interviewed for this book—Republicans and Democrats, African-Americans and Jews. They all blamed Jarrett for keeping the president isolated even from those whose good opinion he needed the most.

This included the White House press corps, who found the Obama administration largely impenetrable. Journalists covering the president were like prisoners in Plato's cave: they watched shadows projected on the wall and believed they were viewing reality. Perhaps no reporter better insinuated herself into the White House than the *New York Times'* Jodi Kantor, who did more than thirty interviews with current and former White House staff for her book *The Obamas*. But when asked if she had ever seen the Obamas' White House private quarters, Kantor replied: "No. I can't even name a journalist who has ever been up there under the Obama watch...."

"Before Valerie left Chicago, we had a talk," said Hermene Hartman, the publisher of *N'DIGO*. "At the time, I was president of the African-American business group called ABLE, which had given significant dollars to Barack and had met with him every three to six months when he was a United States senator. And I wanted to continue that connection between us 'Day One People' and Barack. But Valerie said to me, 'I will meet with six people, but I won't meet with all thirty of the people in ABLE and listen to them bellyache.' And I said, 'We don't want to bellyache, we just want to talk. Let's talk about some boards we might be interested in and some appointments.' But she wouldn't relent. We thought she would stay connected to Barack's black base in Chicago. It didn't happen."

"Some of my friends who gave money to Obama in 2008 complain to me that they never hear from him, that he doesn't call them," a prominent figure in Chicago's Jewish community told me. "Well, he doesn't call me either. He never picks up the phone and calls me. He's not like Bill Clinton or Hillary Clinton, who picked up the phone just to chat with you. Barack Obama isn't that kind of warm, fuzzy guy. He's cooler than that, a bit detached. He doesn't put his arm around you and slap you on the back. He's not a glad-hander. I wish he would call me, but that's not the kind of guy he is."

———

There was no love lost between Jarrett and Emanuel when he was the president's chief of staff. Jarrett was aware that Emanuel had tried to block her appointment to the White House staff, and Emanuel knew that Jarrett didn't have much use for his one-hand-washes-the-other style of politicking. Blunt and famously profane, Emanuel is an unsentimental realist who operated as Obama's "legislative brain." When it came to dealing with Congress, Emanuel was in favor of cutting deals and putting up numbers on the scoreboard. It was his job to give the president clear-eyed advice on how to get things done and to apprise him of the cost and benefits of his actions.

However, at almost every turn, Emanuel was thwarted by Jarrett, who functioned along with David Axelrod as Obama's "political brain." Axelrod and Jarrett were charter members of the Cult of Obama; they had drunk deeply of the Obama Kool-Aid. They made certain that the president remained true to his roots as a big-spending, big-government liberal. When Obama retired in the evening to the Family Quarters, he would often turn to Jarrett and say, "*Rahm thinks this is the practical thing for me to do. What do you think the right thing to do is?*"

"There are always separate legislative and political operations going on in every White House," said Billy Tauzin, a veteran Washington lobbyist, who is often described as "a master of politics and policy." "In previous administrations," he said, "there's usually been a coherent meld of these two operations, some sort of broad strategy that was being managed. But that didn't happen in the Obama White House under Emanuel and Jarrett.

"I haven't seen such incoherence in the White House since Jimmy Carter," Tauzin continued. "Whenever the legislative team struck a clear path, a clear understanding and agreement with the leaders in Congress, the political team didn't bother to track it or know about it. They acted as if they were in a completely different paradigm. They ran on a totally different track. That's one of the reasons there's been such frustration among Democrats as well as Republicans in Congress. They don't sense any coherence. The only thing consistent in this White House is that politics always trumps legislative policy. The major goal is whipping your opponent."

In the bitter fights between Jarrett and Emanuel, Obama frequently sided with Jarrett and ignored Emanuel's advice. For instance, though Emanuel warned the president time and again that he didn't have the votes to ram a comprehensive, single-payer healthcare bill through Congress, Jarrett, along with David Axelrod and First Lady Michelle Obama, persuaded the president to go for broke and side with Speaker of the House Nancy Pelosi and her gaggle of leftwing Democrats. Just as Jarrett and her ideological compatriot Axelrod failed to foresee the emergence of the Tea Party, they didn't understand that an enormously complex Rube Goldberg machine like ObamaCare needed to be explained to the public in simple terms.

Emanuel tangled with Jarrett over her effort to put the prestige of the presidency behind Chicago's bid for the 2016 Summer

Olympics. Emanuel was suspicious of Jarrett's motives; he believed she was working on behalf of her old boss, Mayor Daley, and his political cronies, who stood to benefit from the billions of dollars that would be spent on construction, tourism, sponsorships, and advertising. That idea seemed to be lost on the president.

Always the pragmatist, Emanuel urged Obama to leave the Olympic crusade to others and deal instead with pressing national issues, such as skyrocketing unemployment, which was then reaching 10 percent. But Obama ignored Emanuel's entreaties and sided once again with Jarrett, who then persuaded First Lady Michelle Obama to fly with her to Copenhagen and make a dramatic presentation to the International Olympic Committee. "There won't be a dry eye in the room," said Jarrett, sounding shockingly naïve. "I'm sure that it will touch the hearts of each of the IOC members."

"The White House staff didn't want this to happen," said someone who was present during the debates over the Olympics. "They thought it was a loser, and that it would be of no value to the president and his office. What's more, you never let the president go abroad without knowing the outcome in advance. But Valerie had a lot of relationships in Chicago—business and political—and she was still tied in with Mayor Daley."

When it became apparent that the voting in Copenhagen was going to be dicey, Jarrett dropped the first lady as Chicago's chief spokesperson. Instead, she turned to the president for help, arguing that he was "the best brand in the world" and that only his star power and brilliant rhetorical skills could carry the day with IOC members, especially those from African nations. Easily flattered, Obama thought he could prevail by the force of his personality, and he flew off to Copenhagen, where he made an impassioned plea to the assembled IOC members. However, just as Emanuel feared, when the votes were tallied, the Olympic games were awarded to Rio de Janeiro, not Chicago, which finished fourth of four candidate cities. The loss dealt a stinging blow to Obama's international standing.

Jarrett was on the wrong side of several other consequential issues, not the least of which was her stand on Solyndra, the California solar company that went belly up and cost American taxpayers half a billion dollars. Shortly before Obama paid a visit to Solyndra, which had received a $535 million taxpayer-funded loan guarantee, Steve Westly, a prominent venture capitalist and member of Obama's 2008 national finance committee, wrote Jarrett: "A number of us are concerned that the president is visiting Solyndra. There is an increasing concern about the company because their auditors... have issued a [warning] letter.... Many of us believe the company's cost structure will make it difficult for them to survive long term."

Westly wasn't alone in warning Jarrett about Solyndra. Lawrence Summers, the director of the president's National Economic Council, opposed the administration's loan guarantees to Solyndra, writing in a 2009 email that "the government is a crappy venture capitalist." Nonetheless, Jarrett gave her stamp of approval to Obama's visit to the Bay area solar company, where he used words that would come back to haunt him: "The true engine of economic growth will always be companies like Solyndra." Five months later, the company filed for bankruptcy, making it the third U.S. solar manufacturer to fail in a month. As of this writing, Solyndra was under FBI investigation for accounting fraud.

Why did Jarrett ignore the warnings from Steve Westly and Larry Summers? "The process for this particular loan guarantee began under President Bush," said White House spokesman Eric Schultz, ignoring the fact that the Bush administration ultimately rejected the loan. A more honest answer to the question could be found in Valerie Jarrett's Chicago connections, especially her close ties to the George Kaiser Family Foundation, which controlled 35.7 percent of Solyndra. The foundation had made a sizable donation to the University of Chicago Medical Center, where Jarrett once served as chairwoman and where one of Obama's best friends, Eric Whitaker, is currently executive vice president. Billionaire George Kaiser, one of Obama's top 2008 campaign fundraising bundlers, visited the White House no fewer than sixteen times, and Jarrett herself met at least three times with Solyndra lobbyists, who pushed for government assistance.

Jarrett's dubious judgment on Solyndra had one unintended consequence: it focused renewed attention on Obama's wrongheaded and naïve approach to government stimulus spending on green energy projects. Even Brad Jones of Redpoint Ventures, an investment firm with financial connections to Solyndra, saw the error of Obama's ways. "The allocation of spending to clean energy is haphazard; the government is just not well equipped to decide which companies should get the money and how much," Jones wrote Larry Summers. "One of our solar companies [Solyndra] with revenues of less than $100 million (and not yet profitable) received a government loan of $580 million; while that is good for us, I can't imagine it's a good way for the government to use tax-payer money."

———

Jarrett's lack of judgment in domestic affairs was matched by her inexperience in international and military affairs. She was out of her depth during the Obama administration's nearly year-long internal debate over how to deal with CIA intelligence that Osama bin Laden was hiding in plain sight in Pakistan.

The Defense Department calculated there was a 40 to 60 percent chance that Osama bin Laden was living in a compound in Abbottabad, less than a mile from the Pakistan Military Academy. The way the compound was built plus the human intelligence the United States had on the ground led the intelligence community to conclude that the compound was at the very least a high-value target. Secretary of Defense Robert Gates wanted to drop bombs on it and obliterate it.

The CIA argued that, whatever the risks, if the target was as valuable as the intelligence apparatus said it was, then there was no sense in wiping it out. The CIA didn't want to lose the valuable intelligence the compound might contain.

Though Jarrett did not attend meetings in the Situation Room, she privately urged the president not to send in a Navy SEAL team. She told Obama that the raid could turn out to be a replay of 1980's Desert One, when President Jimmy Carter's effort to rescue American hostages in Iran backfired so badly that it helped doom the Carter presidency.

In this case, Obama didn't listen to Jarrett. He believed strongly in what the CIA told him, and decided to send in the Navy SEAL team to capture or kill Osama bin Laden. It was a brave act, but Obama had at least one other motive: he was worried about what voters might think if they became aware he had had a chance to get Osama bin Laden and hadn't taken it.

———————

Neither the president nor his closest advisers came to Washington with experience managing a large staff, and they failed to hire a team of experienced people who knew how to run things in the nation's capital. As a result, many of the Chicagoans who staff the West Wing, including Valerie Jarrett, are strangers in a strange land. In this atmosphere of callowness and insularity, the Obama White House has assumed the trappings of a royal court.

"There is a tremendous amount of jockeying in the White House under Barack Obama, people hoping to push other people out of their positions, fighting over stupid stuff," a former high-ranking member of the staff told me. "This fighting is not built around flattering the king and queen. It's about arousing suspicion in their minds. If the king and queen feel that they need someone to look out for them, it makes them more dependent. They want to know who is really behind them? Who's really their friend? What is the Washington community saying? What is the black community saying?

"In all of this, Valerie Jarrett is both the arsonist and the fire-fighter," this person continued. "She has been able to spread her tentacles into every nook and cranny of the executive branch of government. She creates problems so she can say to the president and first lady, 'I would do anything for you; I would put everything at risk to show you how trustworthy I am.' The president and to a lesser degree the first lady are worried about big stuff, which means that they must depend more and more on the people around them.

"Valerie creates fear. She keeps the Obamas off-balance and keeps them coming back to her. She makes sure that a lot of other people don't have access. She keeps old friends and supporters away. If she can't control you—what you're going to say to the president and the first lady, the issues you're going to push—then you're not going to get in. Only the people she feels she can control can get in. The people who are given access are beholden to Valerie. Every one of the current crop of people in the East Wing are her friends. They think they owe their lives to her.

"Fear is the operative word. When people on the staff hear that Valerie's in the Family Quarters, it scares them. 'What is she saying to the president and first lady about me? Is she giving me credit for what I've done? Is she distorting what I've said?' Valerie tells everyone that she's going up to the Family Quarters, even if she's only delivering a letter."

CHAPTER 11

THE WRATH OF MICHELLE

My staff worries a lot more about what the First Lady thinks than they worry about what I think, on a full range of issues.

—Barack Obama

O f all the ways the mainstream media have kowtowed to the Obamas, none has been more disgraceful than their coverage of Barack's marriage to Michelle. Typically, he is portrayed as the contented husband who is in total sync with his wife. She's depicted as an advocate for military families, a crusader against childhood obesity, the devoted mom to Sasha and Malia, and a creature of serene domesticity.

In this storybook rendering of the Obamas' marriage, Barack runs the country while Michelle keeps him grounded and takes care of the home. When they lay their heads down on their pillows at night, she might turn to him and offer a few household hints on how things could be managed a little better in the White House. But other than that—at least according to this version—Michelle is no Hillary Clinton. She's a traditional, hands-off first lady.

Recently, this insipid portrait of Michelle Obama has undergone some sorely needed revision. In *The Obamas,* by *New York Times* Washington correspondent Jodi Kantor, a mainstream journalist acknowledges for the first time that Michelle is in fact an unrecognized force in her husband's administration. As Kantor writes: "She was sometimes harder on her husband's team than he was, eventually urging him to replace them, and the tensions grew so severe that one top adviser erupted in a meeting in 2010, cursing the absent first lady."

In reaction to Kantor's book, the White House PR machine mounted a swift and vigorous campaign to re-sanitize Michelle's image. The first lady herself went on TV and, in an interview with Gayle King of CBS *This Morning,* declared: "That's been an image that people have tried to paint of me since the day Barack announced—that I'm some angry black woman."

Jodi Kantor's journalistic amour propre was deeply wounded by the charge of racism. She defended her portrayal of Michelle, pointing out that she hadn't cast the first lady as an angry black woman. "Those words aren't in the book," said Kantor. "There's nothing that implies she is. She is portrayed as a very strong woman.... [Barack Obama] came to Washington on top of the Earth and has kind of been descending to Earth ever since, and Mrs. Obama came here with low expectations and exceeded them."

Michelle exceeded expectations. Indeed, a close reading of the book makes it abundantly clear that Kantor admires the first lady and thinks she has done a terrific job in a difficult role. The book may expose some of the first lady's sharper edges and hint at her true role in the White House, but the author hardly lands a punch.

So, what is the truth about Michelle?

Not since Bill and Hillary Clinton burst upon the political scene more than twenty years ago, promising two for the price of one, have we seen anything like Barack and Michelle's partnership of power in the White House. There is, however, a crucial difference between the Clintons and the Obamas. Whereas the Clintons were open and aboveboard about their co-presidency— boasting that Hillary was an equal partner with Bill—the Obamas have been careful to hide the fact that Michelle is the president's most important political adviser and the one he listens to above all others before he makes major decisions.

Their stealth co-presidency has obscured a vital fact— namely, that the Obamas share a sense of entitlement, an attitude that they know best, a contempt for the political process, and a callow understanding of the way the world works. Their common worldview drives the president's agenda and has brought the United States ever closer to a European-style socialist welfare state.

By any measure, Michelle Obama is further to the Left politically than her husband. And that's saying a lot. Take the president's trillion-dollar, budget-busting healthcare legislation: while presidential advisers Rahm Emanuel, David Axelrod, and Vice President Joe Biden all urged Obama to scale back on the unpopular bill, Michelle encouraged her husband's messianic impulses, urging him to save America from its wicked ways and press ahead, no matter what the consequences.

"The health care overhaul fit perfectly with their shared sense of mission—their joint idea that the president's career was not about pursuing day-to-day political victories but the kinds of fundamental changes they had sought since they were young," Kantor writes in *The Obamas*.

> This was Michelle's most profound influence on the Obama presidency: the sense of purpose she shared with her husband, the force of her worldview, her passionate beliefs about access, opportunity, and fairness; her readiness to do what was unpopular and pay political costs. Every day he met with advisers who emphasized the practical realities of Washington, who reminded him of poll numbers; he spent his nights with Michelle, who talked about moral imperatives, aides said, who reminded him again and again that they were there to do good, to avoid being distracted by political noise, to be bold....

The first lady's handlers have painted a picture of Michelle as a woman who, throughout her marriage, has done everything in her power to *discourage* her husband from running for public office. This view of Michelle is accepted as gospel among the chattering classes on the East and West Coasts, where liberal conventional wisdom holds that Michelle Obama hates politics and politicians.

"I didn't come to politics with a lot of faith in the process," she has said. "I didn't believe that politics was structured in a way that could solve real problems for people." Another time she said, "I am tired of just giving the political process over to the privileged. To the wealthy. To people with the right daddy." And of course there was her famous remark to Carla Bruni-Sarkozy, France's first lady, that her life in the White House was "hell—I can't stand it." (Michelle denied having made the remark, but few believed her.)

Conventional wisdom aside, Michelle's comments raise some puzzling questions:

- If she hates politics so much, why did she hitch her wagon to a political star like Barack Obama, who had an insatiable ambition to achieve national public office?

- What can she possibly have against a political system that has brought her family nothing but financial fortune and unimaginable comfort, made her a celebrity as America's first black first lady, and put her on *Forbes'* list of the World's Most Powerful Women?

- How can she say she hates politics when she is playing a major role raising money and delivering speeches on behalf of her husband's 2012 reelection campaign?

Political wives have always found something to complain about. After all, politics is a blood sport, and spouses end up with many of the same wounds as their husbands. However, based on my reporting, I believe that Michelle's scornful attitude toward politics has far less to do with her life as a political wife than it has to do with deep-seated grievances that she has carried over from her childhood.

Although you wouldn't know it from the way she talks now, Michelle LaVaughn Robinson came from a family steeped in politics. The Robinsons depended for their modest livelihood and fragile perch in the middle class on political connections. Her father, Fraser Robinson III, was a precinct captain in the political machine run by the original Mayor Daley—Richard J.—who was the last of the big city bosses. In exchange for working as a precinct captain in old man Daley's corrupt Democratic machine, Fraser Robinson was given a low-level patronage job as a Chicago city pump operator.

Precinct captains were the machine's foot soldiers at the neighborhood level. They delivered votes on Election Day and, if necessary, stuffed ballot boxes. When Michelle was growing up, the machine was dominated by Irish Catholics like Daley who resisted racial integration and gave Chicago the reputation of being the most segregated city in the North.

Despite Fraser Robinson's lifetime devotion to the regular Democratic organization, he and black folks like him were treated as second-class citizens. The South Side where the Robinson family lived had the worst schools in the city. When it snowed, their streets didn't get plowed. Uncollected garbage piled up on their sidewalks. Fraser, who suffered from a painful case of multiple sclerosis and needed two canes to walk, never missed a day of work. He hobbled about the neighborhood and listened to people tell him that they needed a Parkway fence or another cop on the beat. But he didn't receive the raises and promotions that customarily came to white precinct captains.

Fraser was a proud man who never complained about his disability or treatment. But Michelle grew up feeling sorry for him. She resented the political power structure that failed to recognize her beloved father's value. At night, when the Robinson family gathered around the dinner table, they often talked about how it was necessary to game the system in order to get along. If you wanted to hold on to your steady job in Mayor Daley's Chicago, you had to soil your hands in Democratic politics. As far as Michelle was concerned, however, the system was stacked against black people and she didn't want any part of it.

According to friends, Michelle was ashamed that her father worked in such a dirty business. Though she and Santita Jackson, the daughter of the Reverend Jesse Jackson Sr., were inseparable friends at the Whitney Young Magnet High School, Michelle never admitted to Santita that her father was a precinct captain. Young Michelle spent many afternoons in the Jackson household, but she kept her father's job as a precinct captain a secret from her best friend.

———

Michelle's cynical attitude toward politics was encouraged by her mother, Marian Robinson. Friends and neighbors say that

Michelle got her attitude and biting sarcasm from her formidable mother. In the words of her son, Craig Robinson, currently the men's basketball coach at Oregon State University, Marian was "a force to be reckoned with"—a phrase that is echoed today by people who work with Michelle Obama in the White House.

In his memoir, *A Game of Character*, Craig tells a story about his mother that's worth repeating for the light it casts on the formative influence that Marian Robinson had on her children. Once, a policeman stopped Craig and accused him of stealing the bike he was riding. "Instead of taking me at my word, [the policeman] insisted on loading the bike into the back of his cruiser and driving me home so he could speak to my parents," Craig wrote.

> From downstairs I called up to Mom that the policeman had accused me of stealing a bike, and when she came outside, I saw a look on her face that I'd never seen before. "Go on inside, Craig," she said, barely glancing at me but steeling her eyes on the officer, preparing to read him the riot act. I stood watching from the front screened-in porch, and she must have talked to that policeman for forty-five minutes. Then he pulled the bike out of the trunk, set it on the curb, and drove off.... But that wasn't the end of it. The next day, Marian Robinson paid a visit to the station house. And the day after that, the policeman came to our home and apologized to me.

Like her mother, Michelle doesn't let sleeping dogs lie. She often behaves as though others have let her down and she's better than they are. Even on the rare occasions when people *do* meet her exalted standards—such as when whites came out and voted in large numbers for her husband in the Democratic presidential primary—Michelle can't help but let her sense of grievance show through. Thus her most notorious remark, which she made in Milwaukee, Wisconsin, on February 18, 2008: "For the first time in my adult life I am proud of my country because it feels like hope is finally making a comeback."

Everyone in Michelle's family is afraid of her. "My mom and I and my dad, before he died, we were all worried about, 'Oh, my god, my sister's never getting married because each guy she'd meet, she's gonna chew him up, spit him out,'" Craig Robinson said. "So I was thinking, Barack says one wrong thing and she is going to jettison him. She'll fire a guy in a minute, just fire him."

Later, after Michelle and Barack married, Craig was asked if his brother-in-law used a nicotine patch to help him quit smoking. To which Craig laughingly replied: "Michelle Obama—that's one hell of a patch right there!"

Despite her fiery reputation among friends and family, stories about Michelle's temper have rarely appeared in the liberal mainstream media, which have gone out of their way to protect her. A reporter has to dig hard to find people who are willing to talk about their encounters with Michelle. Here are three first-hand accounts from people who have witnessed the Wrath of Michelle:

From a Harvard Law School classmate of Barack Obama's, who asked to remain anonymous: "When Michelle came to visit

Barack at Harvard, he was living in a rundown basement apartment in a working-class neighborhood called Somerville, where
he socialized almost exclusively with other African-Americans.
The furniture was cobbled together from god-knows-where, and
you'd sit on a chair and it would break. He had an old Toyota,
which Michelle drove around. It used to break down, and they
argued about it all the time.

"Barack was treated specially by a lot of people at Harvard,
and Michelle found that hard to handle. His ego was pretty
inflated, and Michelle would fly in from Chicago, and the first
thing she'd do was take him down a peg or two. She laughed at
his pretentiousness.

"But she couldn't change the fact that he was immensely
popular. He was handsome and successful and incredibly well
spoken. His classmates, black and white, flocked to him. He was
a guy with a slick way with words, and women especially were
attracted to him. I remember one time Michelle showed up unex-
pectedly at his desk in the library, and found him surrounded by
women. It was terrible timing, and Barack looked like the pro-
verbial cat who swallowed the canary; he had a really pained
expression on his face. He had been working his ass off studying,
and girls that he knew from classes happened by just as Michelle
showed up. Michelle was so damn mad that she put a hand on
his shoulder in a possessive way, then gave him this disdainful
look, turned on her heels, and marched out without a word, her
heels clicking on the marble floors. She went back to Chicago.

"Another time, the same sort of thing happened at his Somerville apartment. She came in and found him with some women,

black women. Michelle threw a fit and left. He followed her down the street, Charles Street, begging her to stay.

"I think she drove a lot of Barack's friends away. If she didn't find them helpful, she would simply be rude. She and Barack had constant fights, and they could be incredibly exasperated with each other. Frankly, I was surprised the relationship lasted through law school. I remember thinking, *This isn't going to work.*

"For a while, Michelle was very unsure about the relationship. Barack seemed to have his life the way he liked it, and she wanted to remake him. But soon after Barack graduated from law school, and the world started beating a path to his door, Michelle decided he was going to go far, and she insisted that he marry her. He got cold feet, but Michelle wouldn't take no for an answer. She was a formidable woman even back then."

From Charles Thomas, a veteran political reporter for Chicago's ABC News affiliate ABC 7: "I accompanied Obama on a trip he made to Africa in 2006, and when he returned, *Time* magazine did a cover story on him with the cover line Why Barack Obama Could be the Next President. The morning *Time*'s story appeared, Michelle had a previously scheduled interview on our local ABC TV news show. Her people told our people that we couldn't ask her about the *Time* cover story. But my editor told me to go down to the green room and see if she would comment about it.

"So I went down to the green room. I asked, 'Michelle, how are the kids? We want to talk to you about the *Time* magazine piece.' And she rose up out of her chair. She's a lot taller than I am. And she put her hand on her hip and glared down at me. Waving her forefinger at me, she said, 'Charles, don't you try that shit with me or I'll walk out of here!'"

From African-American talk-show host Tavis Smiley: "About five years ago, I published a book, *The Covenant with Black America*, and I got PBS to let me moderate a prime-time nationally televised debate in which the candidates were questioned only by journalists of color on issues of interest principally to people of color. All the candidates showed up. All the big-time Hillary supporters and all the big Obama people were there. The debate took place at Howard University, and afterward the media said Hillary had killed Obama and gotten the most applause.

"After the debate, with the cameras still rolling, the candidates were on the stage shaking hands. And in the midst of all this, Michelle Obama comes up on the stage and grabs me by the back of my jacket, and yanks me backward, and gets in my face. 'Why are you messing with Barack,' she yells at me. This is in front of the auditorium with thousands of people. 'You were unfairly tough on Barack,' she says. 'You should know as a black man what he's up against and what he's trying to do.' And she proceeds to lay into me. I had to leave her standing there because it was getting really testy."

If Michelle ever had any reservations about Barack's grandiose political dreams, they didn't come from her qualms about politics, but from her belief that he wasn't aiming high enough. For example, when he ran for a seat in the Illinois state legislature, Michelle told him that it was "too small time." Remarks a friend of the Obamas: "They both already knew so many important people [and] she just wanted him to go straight to the national stage."

For the first several years of their marriage, Michelle and Barack lived in a flat in a lower-middle-class neighborhood. But after Barack's memoir *Dreams from My Father* hit the bestseller lists and he joined the United States Senate, the couple moved to a million-dollar mansion, and Michelle landed a cushy job at the University of Chicago Medical Center with a salary of $317,000 a year.* It hardly seemed a coincidence that Valerie Jarrett was the medical center's chairwoman, and that a hospital board member, Kelly R. Welsh, was an executive vice president at Northern Trust Company, which had extended the Obamas a $1.3 million home mortgage.

Chicago-style cronyism marked Michelle's tenure at the University of Chicago Medical Center. Given all her righteous talk about "fundamental change," "access," "opportunity," and "fairness," everyone expected Michelle to promote programs to assist the underprivileged denizens of the black South Side. Instead, she helped launch a program, dubbed the South Side Health Collaborative, to save the hospital millions of dollars by redirecting poor and uninsured patients from its emergency room to surrounding

---

* Michelle's actual annual salary, between the university and serving on six boards of directors, including Walmart, approached $500,000.

community hospitals in the South Side. The University of Chicago's Medical Center beds were reserved for prosperous patients who used profitable procedures.

The president of the American College of Emergency Physicians, Dr. Nick Jouriles, released a statement saying Michelle's program came "dangerously close to 'patient dumping,' a practice made illegal by the emergency Medical Labor and Treatment Act, and reflected an effort to 'cherry pick' wealthy patients over poor."

To deflect criticism, Michelle gave the program a more appealing name, the Urban Health Initiative, and hired a public relations firm co-owned by David Axelrod, who was soon to become Barack Obama's chief strategist for his presidential campaign. Axelrod's job was to sell the Urban Health Initiative to community skeptics like Edward Novak, president of Chicago's Sacred Heart Hospital, who described Axelrod's PR efforts to justify the program as "bull." As for Michelle's moral imperatives, a survey by the polling firm Peter D. Hart Research Associates noted: "More than a few staff members—particularly medical staff—express strongly worded concern or disappointment with UCMC in its commitment to the community."

Though Michelle now likes to pretend that she plays no part in personnel decisions or in formulating policy in the White House, the facts tell quite a different story. Michelle's aides meet regularly with the president's senior communications team and select public events that will maximize and reinforce the Obamas' joint message.

According to a New York State Democratic Party official, "Michelle certainly played a role" in selecting Joe Biden, instead of Hillary Clinton, as her husband's vice presidential running mate. "Do you really want Bill and Hillary just down the hall from you in the White House?" Michelle asked her husband. "Could you live with that?" He couldn't.

Also, according to one of Barack's closest confidants, Michelle "was one of the strongest voices" arguing for the appointment of Federal Appeals Court Judge Sonia Sotomayor to replace retiring Associate Justice David Souter on the Supreme Court. "The First Lady thought Sotomayor had all those... qualities her husband was looking for in an appointee," the confidant said. "Barack has always listened to what she has to say."

Michelle rarely conveys her opinions directly to the president's staff. When she is upset about something, she generally turns to her best friend, Valerie Jarrett, and makes Jarrett the messenger of her displeasure. Such was the case in the fall of 2010 when the story broke that Michelle had told Carla Bruni-Sarkozy that she "can't stand" life in the White House, that it was "hell." Robert Gibbs, Obama's longtime press secretary, worked furiously to put out the fire and get the Élysée Palace in Paris to issue a denial. He accomplished his task, but apparently he didn't do so quickly enough to satisfy Michelle Obama.

The next day at the president's 7:30 a.m. staff meeting, Valerie Jarrett let it be known that the first lady was "dissatisfied" with the way Gibbs had handled the matter. As Jodi Kantor recounts in *The Obamas*, Gibbs blew his stack.

"Fuck this, that's not right, I've been killing myself on this, where's this coming from?" he bellowed. "What is it she has concerns about? What did she say to you?"

Jarrett offered a vague response.

"What the fuck do you mean?" Gibbs said. "Did you ask her?"

Jarrett explained that the denial from the Élysée Palace had not come fast enough.

"Why is she talking to *you* about it?" Gibbs demanded to know. "If she has a problem she should talk to me!"

"You shouldn't talk that way," Jarrett said.

"You don't know what the fuck you're talking about," Gibbs said.

"The first lady would not believe you're speaking this way," Jarrett said.

"Then fuck her, too!" Gibbs said.

Michelle's interference in White House policy was also a touchy subject with Rahm Emanuel when he was chief of staff. He and the first lady had never gotten along. They were the yin and yang of the White House, frequently on opposite sides of an issue. They gave each other a wide berth, but still grated on each other's nerves. Emanuel particularly resented the fact that the first lady sent scolding emails to Alyssa Mastromonaco, the president's director of scheduling, and that these emails were passed around the White House, undercutting his authority. When the *Washington Post* ran a story saying that Emanuel was trying to save the president from his amateurish inclinations—"Why Obama Needs Rahm at the Top"—it was assumed that the chief of staff, who was famous for calling reporters, had leaked the story. As a result, his stock fell to a new low with Michelle.

In January 2010, the Democrats lost Edward Kennedy's Senate seat from Massachusetts, costing the party its filibuster-proof majority and dooming Obama's chances of passing legislation for a government-run, single-payer healthcare system. Michelle was fit to be tied. She couldn't understand why the president's advisers had failed to read the political tea leaves in Massachusetts, or why they had sent Obama to Massachusetts at the eleventh hour on a fruitless mission to save Martha Coakley, the inept Democratic candidate. The whole thing smacked of amateurism, and according to several sources, Michelle told the president that he needed a new team of advisers, starting with Rahm Emanuel.

"She feels as if our rudder isn't set right," the president told his aides. When Emanuel heard that, he strode into the Oval Office and offered his resignation. It was turned down. But by then Emanuel's days were numbered.

From time to time, Michelle did impulsive, silly things that spoiled her carefully crafted image. At such moments, her handlers were forced to launch one of their frequent PR makeovers. This practice first became apparent right after Barack Obama won the Democratic nomination in June 2008. Voters still held serious reservations about his wife, who seemed to take pleasure in demeaning the candidate and mocking his "stinky" morning breath.

As Kate Betts wrote in *Everyday Icon: Michelle Obama and the Power of Style*:

> Her approval rating lingered at 43 percent. Something had to be done. Political dreams have been dashed on less daunting obstacles than an unpopular spouse. With a savvy sense of what was necessary, and no hint of strain, in a matter of weeks Michelle Obama appeared to make a midcourse correction. She changed the content and tone of her speeches. She changed the way she dressed. She replaced the corporate armor of sleek jackets and pantsuits with soft cardigans and June Cleaver-esque 1950s-style floral print dresses. On the surface it looked as if Michelle Obama was swapping Power Woman for Power Wife....
>
> As Michelle began to substitute homey anecdotes about tucking her kids into bed at night for stump speeches about public policy, she made parallel adjustments to her wardrobe, softening her look and enhancing the idea of accessibility through her clothing.... Her approval ratings started to rise. At the end of August [2009] they had climbed to 53 percent.

Another example of Michelle's impulsive, narcissistic nature was her decision to go on a lavish vacation to Spain in the summer of 2010, at the height of the Great Recession, even though practically her entire staff advised against it. She overruled them and flew off on an Air Force 757 along with three shifts of uniformed plainclothes agents and military personnel. Her security entourage numbered seventy people. Her vast army of support personnel checked into the Villa Padierna Palace Hotel in Marbella, a five-star resort on the Spanish Costa del Sol. The trip cost American taxpayers several hundred thousand dollars, and the backlash was harsh and immediate. A column by Andrea Tantaros in the *New York Daily News* was headlined: "Material Girl Michelle Obama Is a Modern-Day Marie Antoinette on a Glitzy Spanish Vacation."

Though the trip to Spain garnered most of the publicity, it was hardly Michelle's only foray into expensive vacations. Between August 2010 and August 2011, she spent a total of forty-two days on vacation—or one out of every nine days. (During the same period of time, the number of Americans on food stamps increased from thirty-two to forty-six million.)

In February 2012, just weeks after a seventeen-day Christmas vacation in Hawaii, Michelle decided she needed another break. With gas prices at an historic winter high, the government struggling to cut the federal deficit, and many American families forgoing their annual holiday vacations, Michelle thumbed her nose at political convention and jetted off with Sasha and Malia on Presidents' Day weekend for the upmarket ski slopes of Aspen, Colorado. "Several people have known about the 'low-key' vacation, with the Secret Service in town for the past few days scoping out places for the family to relax and enjoy what the resort has to offer," wrote *Aspen Daily News* columnist Carolyn Sackariason.

"Pritkin County Sheriff Joe DiSalvo confirmed that he has met with the Secret Service and has loaned seven deputies to help protect the first lady and her family."

The question naturally arises: Why would someone who is as politically savvy as Michelle Obama do such foolish things?

The answer seems to lie in Michelle's personality, which is acquisitive and materialistic by nature. For her forty-fourth birthday, Obama bought his wife something she had long coveted—a set of diamond stud earrings. He spent $5,000. She promptly returned them in exchange for bigger diamonds that cost $12,000.

"Michelle has expensive tastes," writes Carol Felsenthal in chicagomag.com. "It was she who wanted to trade up from their two-bedroom condominium on the first floor of a three-story walkup, for which they had paid $277,500 in 1993, to the $1.65 million six-bedroom Georgian revival Kenwood mansion that landed them in a deal with the wife of Tony Rezko, the convicted felon and fundraiser/fixer...."

As a high-maintenance woman, Michelle feels right at home in the White House. "It's a cool time in her life," says a journalist who is assigned to follow the first lady full time. "She doesn't have to work hard; she has more help; she's treated like a queen; she never has to worry about money again. She has a contract to write a book about a year in the life of the White House garden.

"Nowadays," continues the journalist, "Michelle doesn't have much stuff to nag Barack about. After all, he's home for dinner most nights of the week. Her kids are in a good place. She's home when the kids come home. She's shown the girls the world. She has time for tennis lessons and workouts. She spends a good part of the day working out in the gym, picking out her wardrobe, and doing her makeup. She's living in a dream world. You know that old saying, When mom's happy, everyone's happy."

CHAPTER 12

OUT TO LUNCH

---

*Politics is all about relationships, people. A
lot of it's emotional. It's not rocket science.*

—Former White House Chief of Staff William M. Daley

W̲hen Barack Obama appointed Bill Daley as his new chief
of staff in January 2011, the bald, genial Chicagoan was
widely expected to be a welcome change from the ruthlessly
aggressive Rahm Emanuel. A world-class schmoozer and political fixer, Daley was weaned on politics: he is the son of the
legendary Mayor Richard J. Daley and the brother of Mayor
Richard M. Daley. Thanks in large part to his family connections, Bill Daley was appointed as commerce secretary in the
Clinton administration, and later became head of the office of
corporate responsibility for JP Morgan Chase, which in practice

meant he spent a lot of time wining and dining the bank's clients. With Daley's experience in both the public and private sectors, and his genuinely warm personality, it was hoped that he would smooth Obama's frayed relationships with the business community and Congress, and bring a grownup, centrist sensibility to a White House that was populated by a crew of cloistered leftwing amateurs.

It didn't happen.

What everyone in the White House had overlooked was that Daley had little legislative experience. Predictably enough, his honeymoon lasted less than a year—a tumultuous year in which he failed to help Obama reach a bipartisan grand bargain with the House of Representatives on reducing the federal budget deficit, and allowed the president to engage in a degrading mud-wrestle with congressional Republicans over raising the debt ceiling.

These raucous ideological arguments left Obama looking weaker than ever, and Valerie Jarrett—who was expert at enhancing her power by finding fault with others—pointed a finger of blame at Daley for failing to protect the president from the political fallout. After getting an earful of anti-Daley static, Obama lost faith in his chief of staff and transferred most of his management responsibilities to Pete Rouse, a longtime aide and political strategist. The hapless Daley was unceremoniously relegated to the sidelines in the West Wing.

By the fall of 2011, as the White House geared up for what was expected to be a massively expensive and brutally negative presidential campaign, Daley felt that his usefulness to the president had come to an end. But he kept his feelings to himself. He deeply resented the role Jarrett had played in his downfall, and before he left his post, he wanted to engage her in one last battle.

A fierce debate had been rocking the White House over a proposal to require church-run hospitals and universities to give their employees free contraception. Jarrett, along with Kathleen Sebelius, the secretary of health and human services, favored the plan. But Bill Daley and Vice President Biden, both Catholics with intimate ties to the church hierarchy, opposed the mandate, arguing that it breached the separation of church and state and would lose the president Catholic votes.

With Biden's approval, Daley secretly arranged an Oval Office meeting between Obama and New York Archbishop Timothy Dolan, the head of the United States Conference of Catholic Bishops, who argued that the policy violated the principle of religious freedom. Daley knew he was running a risk by scheduling such a meeting. Obama didn't like to hear anyone tell him that he was wrong, and White House sources later revealed that the president had felt uncomfortable being put on the spot by Dolan, who would shortly be elevated to cardinal. However, Obama's discomfort was nothing compared to Valerie Jarrett's. She hadn't been informed about the meeting, and when she learned about Daley's end-run, she went to the president and vented her anger.

Obama faced a major rift among his closest advisers on an immensely sensitive social issue. Who should he back? On one side stood Daley, Biden, and Nancy-Ann DeParle, the deputy chief of staff who had coordinated the passage of ObamaCare but opposed the contraceptive mandate because, she argued, it would lose Obama the support of liberal as well as conservative Catholics. On the other side stood Jarrett, Sebelius, and David Plouffe, who had replaced David Axelrod as Obama's senior in-house political adviser, and argued that since most Catholics flouted the church's dictates on birth control, they wouldn't penalize Obama at the ballot box.

Largely lost in the debate was a simple fact: a mandate forcing religious institutions to go against their beliefs and conscience and offer contraception was constitutionally wrong and politically stupid. That, however, didn't stop Obama from announcing he was going ahead with the mandate, thereby pleasing his Democratic base and adding another victory in his crusade to move America to the Left.

His victory dance was short-lived, however. For within a matter of weeks, he had to revise his original proposal to quiet the political storm that he had unleashed.

In January 2012, a disgusted Bill Daley abruptly resigned, embarrassing the president. Obama called a hasty press conference and, grim-faced, announced his new—and fourth, counting Pete Rouse, who served in an interim role between Emanuel and Daley—chief of staff, Jacob Lew, the obscure White House budget director.

It was a new low, even for Barack Obama.

———

The Daley debacle underscored a truth universally acknowledged by Obama's friends and adversaries—namely, that after more than three years in office, his administration was still amateurish and in disarray. The inability of Daley, with all his people skills, to bridge some of the differences between the White House and Congress emphasized just how isolated and out of touch Obama and his team were from the realities of Washington.

"Every modern president, perhaps with the exception of Gerry Ford, entered the White House with a large quotient of self-assurance and arrogance," a top aide to the Republican House leadership told me, speaking on the condition of anonymity. "But what makes this president unique is that he is so beyond that. Not only is he self-assured, the smartest guy in the room, but in his estimation all he has to do is state something and the scales will fall from your eyes. Despite the storyline people create, that he is a thoughtful, non-ideological compromiser, he has a distinct leftist ideology and can't make a decision that takes him out of his comfort zone.

"My first experience with him was in January 2010, just after his State of the Union speech, when we went to the White House for a bicameral meeting in the Cabinet room," the Republican aide continued. "The president said he needed to find common cause on his cap and trade energy policy. He said, 'I've taken on my party by being pro-nuclear, so now you have to give me cap and trade.' By that, he meant he was willing to lift the ban on the construction of nuclear energy sites. But in fact, he hadn't taken any substantive position on nuclear power. It was just words.

"Not long after that, there was another meeting in the Cabinet Room. This time the president said, 'The economy is not doing all that bad. You guys [the Republicans] have to stop being negative.' And [Speaker of the House] John Boehner said, 'Mr. President, the problem with the economy is the uncertainty on taxes, cap and trade, and healthcare. Until there is certainty, businesses are not going to invest.' And the president slapped his hand on the table and said, 'You're WRONG! I talk to CEOs all the time and they tell me the problem is Washington doesn't work.' Of course, by that he meant that Washington didn't work the way *he* wanted it to work.

"He's got so little appreciation and knowledge of how Congress works—that it's an equal branch of government. If you challenge him, he's furious. He gives you the death stare. He has no close relationship with any member of the Senate. And certainly not in the House. John Boehner says that, in his twenty years in Washington, he's been through four administrations, and that this one is completely opaque. He doesn't know who makes the decisions and how they make them in the Obama White House.

"All this goes back to the fact that Obama is a leftist. He doesn't understand that the way to make this town work, both sides have to get up from the table thinking that they've won something. This White House is incapable of doing that."

It wasn't only Republicans who found Barack Obama infuriatingly out of touch. Even the mainstream media, which had fawned over Obama for the better part of three years, began to wake up to the truth.

"This president," wrote the *Washington Post*'s Scott Wilson, "endures with little joy the small talk and back-slapping of retail politics, rarely spends more than a few minutes on a rope line, refuses to coddle even his biggest donors. His relationship with Democrats on Capitol Hill is frosty, to be generous. Personal lobbying on behalf of legislation? He prefers to leave that to Vice President Joe Biden, an old-school political charmer. ...

"Obama's isolation," Wilson continued, "is increasingly relevant as the 2012 campaign takes shape, because it is pushing him toward a reelection strategy that embraces the narrowcast politics he once rejected as beneath him. Now he is focused on securing the support of traditional Democratic allies—minorities, gays, young people, seniors, Jews—rather than on making new friends. ..."

If Obama's reelection strategy depended on the kindness of old friends, he was in for a disappointment. With the exception of union leaders like Andy Stern—the former president of the 2.2 million-member Service Employees International Union, who had visited the White House more than fifty times—most of the president's major supporters had been given the brush-off and were nursing bruised egos. This was especially true of high-profile Democrats like Oprah Winfrey, Caroline Kennedy, and leading members of the Jewish community—all of whom have been snubbed by the Obama White House.

Indeed, one of the most important stories in Washington was just how angry and disillusioned these Democratic luminaries were with the president and first lady. A critical question hovering over the 2012 presidential campaign was whether these one-time friends would return to the Obama fold.

PART III

WITH FRIENDS LIKE THESE

*We walk alone in the world. Friends,
such as we desire, are dreams and fables.*

—Ralph Waldo Emerson

CHAPTER 13

OPRAH'S SACRIFICE

Oprah is from the world of Christmas—
mystical, cheerful, appealing, even beguiling.
She is no policy wonk, but is cast well as a black,
female St. Nick bringing joy to the world. Her
endorsement softens Obama, wraps him up,
and makes of him a Christmas present to America.

—Dick Morris

Shortly after the 2008 presidential election, Oprah Winfrey traveled to Washington, D.C., to nail down an interview for *O, The Oprah Magazine* with Michelle Obama. Oprah expected the president-elect and his wife to give her a reception fit for visiting royalty, and for the occasion, she took along Gayle King, the magazine's editor-at-large and her constant companion.

More than a year and a half had passed since Oprah announced that she was throwing her support behind Barack Obama in his primary race against Hillary Clinton. The endorsement had represented a calculated risk for the queen of daytime television.

It was one thing for her to recommend a book or launch the career of Dr. Phil, but it was quite another for her to back a political candidate. Oprah worried that her audience, which represented a broad economic, cultural, and political spectrum of American women, would resent her becoming a partisan for a political candidate.

As it turned out, a sizable chunk of her audience took offense and stopped watching her show. No sooner had Oprah hit the campaign trail, appearing beside Obama at one primary rally after another, than her personal favorability ratings began to slide, falling from 74 to 66 percent. Her *unfavorable* ratings suffered an even worse fate; they jumped from 17 to 26 percent. Most important, her endorsement of Obama caused a significant drop in the ratings of her TV show and in the rates that she could charge advertisers.

Was the sacrifice worth it? As an entertainer and businesswoman, Oprah had suffered a setback. But she felt proud that she had been instrumental in electing the first black president of the United States, and she believed that she had earned a place in the president-elect's brain trust. As the *New York Times* editorialized: "Her early and enthusiastic endorsement of Senator Obama... played a big role in winning over bit parts of Middle America to the Obama cause." Two economists at the University of Maryland, College Park, estimated that Oprah's endorsement netted Obama 1,015,559 votes and decided the primary election. And the Pew Research Center found that Oprah's appearance on the stage with Obama made him more acceptable to African-American voters, some of whom had wondered if he was "black enough."

During the early weeks of the presidential transition, as Obama stitched together his new White House team, he appeared to embrace Oprah as one of his trusted advisers. When she phoned, he dropped everything and took her call. They huddled over strategy. Of all of Obama's unofficial White House advisers, Oprah had unparalleled access, input, influence, and power.

However, by the time Oprah and Gayle landed in Washington a month after the election, Oprah's relationship with the Obamas had come unglued.

Oprah had tried to ignore the ominous change in tone coming from the Obama transition team. As Barack Obama's inauguration drew near, Oprah's calls to Michelle went unreturned. Instead, Oprah heard from Max Doebler, the newly appointed White House ceremonies coordinator, who told Oprah that she needed to talk to him first about the interview. What's more, Doebler said, Oprah had to run her interview questions past Jeff Stephens, a deputy speechwriter, for prior approval.

"It was a pain as far as Oprah was concerned," said a high-ranking executive of Harpo Studios, Oprah's production company. "Oprah isn't a snob, but she doesn't like having to put up with mid-level clerks. These guys were $75,000-a-year men. Oprah was like, 'Hello, what is this shit!' But she did it; she went to Washington with Gayle and met with both Doebler and Stephens to hash out the details. I was surprised that she went there, hat in hand."

It soon became apparent that something had gone wrong between Oprah and the new administration—or, more precisely, between Oprah and Michelle Obama. The problem seemed to originate from two of Michelle's advisers, Valerie Jarrett and Desirée Rogers, the new White House social secretary. They resented Oprah's meddling in their bailiwick. Among other things, Oprah had a plan to redecorate the Lincoln bedroom. She also had ideas about how Michelle could put more zing into White House social events.

As the person who controlled access to the first couple, Valerie Jarrett saw Oprah as a potential threat to her power. If Oprah went unchecked, she would bypass Valerie and go directly to the president and first lady. What good was it being the gatekeeper if you couldn't lock the gate when you wanted? And so Valerie set about turning Michelle against Oprah. *Oprah was too close to the president… Oprah was acting like* she *was the first lady… Oprah didn't know her place… Oprah was a bad influence….* Valerie advised Michelle to "distance herself" from Oprah and cut her out of the White House inner circle.

It didn't take much to convince Michelle. As Michelle knew only too well, her husband had a compelling need to win the approval of strong women like Oprah. He seemed to be in awe of the talk show host, sometimes giving her advice priority over Michelle's. For instance, Oprah thought that Obama was overexposing himself on television and told him to pull back. Though Michelle disagreed, Obama listened to Oprah and restricted his TV appearances. As far as Michelle was concerned, Oprah's billions and her elite lifestyle disqualified her as an adviser to Barack, who had no truck with wealthy people, except as a source of campaign contributions, and was a redistributionist at heart.

There was another reason for Michelle's negative attitude toward Oprah. "Michelle is very jealous, I would say unusually so," said someone who was very close to Oprah. "Most people after years of marriage have trust and don't follow their husbands around and check on them. Michelle doesn't seem to trust Barack at all. She insists on knowing his every movement and drops in on him at all kinds of odd times. It's been the buzz of the White House. Oprah has gossiped about it and giggled about how obsessive Michelle is. This is what she hears from her friends who work in the East Wing, and, believe me, she has some good sources. Everybody wants to be Oprah's source, and she loves gossip.

"Michelle makes it clear to her inner circle, and this certainly includes Valerie, that she wants women around Barack watched and wants info about who he has an eye for and gets touchy with," this person continued. "The thing is, she knows, like everybody, about JFK's shenanigans, and she thinks, hey, JFK was young and good looking like my guy.

"Michelle talked to Gayle King about it, just talking as friends. She has become much closer to Gayle than to Oprah, to Oprah's anger and surprise. She told Gayle that if she found out her husband was running around she wouldn't keep quiet. Gayle was kind of astonished that she would say that."

———————

Eventually, Oprah got a green light for her interview, and on February 17, 2009, she and Gayle climbed into Oprah's custom-built, $42 million Bombardier Global Express XRS and jetted off to Washington. The women had talked about having Oprah's $335,000 Bentley Azure convertible pick them up at Reagan National Airport and drive them to the White House with the top down, even though it was a cold, cloudy day with the temperature in the thirties. But it occurred to them that Michelle wasn't going to be waiting at the front door of the White House and wouldn't notice their grand entrance.* So they ditched the Bentley idea, and counted on the White House sending a suburban and driver to meet them at the airport. But that didn't happen, either. Instead, Oprah had to pay for a limo ride to the White House.

When they arrived, Oprah and Gayle weren't treated like VIPs; they were made to wait at the security gate like ordinary visitors. Once inside, they had to cool their heels for a long time before they were shown up to the Yellow Oval Room in the family residence, where Michelle finally made an appearance.

"Michelle told Oprah and Gayle what great light the room got," said a Harpo executive who spoke to Oprah later about the meeting. "But it was a grim, overcast, washed-out sort of a day. Michelle also told them how great it was to be waited on by a large staff, as if Oprah wouldn't know about that. And oddly enough, Michelle mentioned that the White House cooks made the best pie in the world. But she didn't offer Oprah or Gayle any. It was almost an act of cruelty. Instead, she served them almonds, not an Oprah fave.

"Michelle seemed to direct her answers and asides to Gayle, rather than Oprah," the Harpo exec continued. "It made both

---

* Aware of Michelle's expensive tastes, Oprah made a point of wearing her $117,000 Cartier Diabolo watch to the White House meeting with the first lady.

Oprah and Gayle very uncomfortable, which may have been the idea. Oprah struck back by asking Michelle whether she and the president were still fighting a lot. Taken aback by such a personal question, Michelle stumbled, then finally managed to say that the marital arguing had been a 'growth point' in their relationship."

Months later, when Michelle announced she was going to devote herself to fighting childhood obesity, Oprah offered to pitch in. She sent word to Michelle that she would love to have her on her TV show, where Michelle could tell millions of viewers about healthy nutrition for their children and families. Oprah also wanted to broadcast a show from the White House on the subject of exercise and weight control.

Once again, Oprah waited in vain for a response from the White House. When an answer finally arrived, it was curt to the point of rudeness: "That wouldn't fit into the First Lady's plans." According to sources for this book, Oprah told Gayle King that she felt like getting Michelle on the phone and really letting her have it. Oprah raged: "Michelle hates fat people and doesn't want me waddling around the White House."

Eventually, Gayle convinced Oprah to let her draft a diplomatic note expressing Oprah's disappointment. But an Oprah aide, who was close to several members of the White House staff, learned that Michelle treated Gayle's letter with scorn. "Oprah only wants to cash in, using the White House as a backdrop for her show to perk up her ratings," Michelle was quoted as telling her staff. "Oprah, with her yo-yo dieting and huge girth, is a terrible role model. Kids will look at Oprah, who's rich and famous and huge, and figure it's okay to be fat."

Oprah went through the roof when she heard about Michelle's remarks. "If Michelle thinks I need more fame and money," said Oprah, "she's nuts."

I asked a White House insider to explain Michelle's animus toward Oprah. "Michelle is furious that her husband makes late-night calls to Oprah, seeking ideas on how to improve his sinking popularity," the source told me. "Michelle thinks he should turn to her, not Oprah, for that kind of advice. What's more, Michelle suspects that at one point Oprah secretly encouraged Hillary to consider a run against Barack in the 2012 Democratic primaries. Barack just laughs at the idea and so does Oprah. But Michelle still believes Oprah has been getting too close to Hillary, whom Michelle calls 'a snake.'"

Nonetheless, the president pushed Michelle, against her will, to make a sort of peace with Oprah in order to get Oprah's endorsement in 2012. Left with little choice, Michelle reluctantly agreed to tape an interview for one of the last *Oprah* TV shows, in May 2011. She sat there through much of the show with her arms folded in a defensive posture across her chest.

———————

Will Oprah support Barack Obama in his second run for the White House? And if so, will she expend the same energy and enthusiasm that she exhibited the first time around?

Those questions could be asked not only of Oprah, but of Obama's other key supporters and fundraisers from the 2008 election. For many of them, disillusionment has replaced the old fire in their belly. Three and a half years of aloofness, non-communication, and dithering amateurism by the president left his old shock troops in a state of shock.

Obama's campaign staff has scrambled to repair the damage and convince these important Democrats that the president will be more considerate of their views in the future. Obama Campaign Headquarters in Chicago has dialed up a charm offensive, and Democrats who hadn't heard from the president for months or even years were showered with sudden invitations to the White House.

Despite all this, rumors persisted that Oprah would sit out the 2012 election. When I asked Gayle King about that, she told me, "Ed, we have every intention of supporting the president for reelection." But the question still remained whether Oprah would run the risk of further alienating her audience by going beyond a verbal endorsement and actively campaigning for Obama.

Since leaving her syndicated talk show and launching OWN, the Oprah Winfrey Network, Oprah has been struggling with anemic ratings. She and her backers have lost tens of millions of dollars and have been searching for new investors. By closely associating herself with Barack Obama, she might complicate her efforts to save OWN. In any case, after suffering repeated snubs from Michelle, it seems likely that this time around, Oprah Winfrey would play it safe and put her business interests before politics.

CHAPTER 14

SNUBBING CAROLINE

I mean, Caroline Kennedy—come on!
She's part of history.

—Michelle Obama

It was toward the end of June 2009, and the weather in Hyannis Port had turned grim and chilling. Senator Edward M. Kennedy, who was suffering from the final stages of incurable brain cancer, had just returned from an excursion on his beloved sailboat, the *Maya*. His wife, Victoria Reggie, was waiting for him in a golf cart at the wind-swept dock. Two burly aides lifted Ted out of the boat and placed him gently beside his wife. The couple then drove to a large tent, where almost one hundred members of the Kennedy clan had gathered near the home of Ethel Kennedy for a birthday party for two of her grandchildren.

"It was a rare gathering of the extended family," the wife of one of Ethel's sons said in an interview for this book. "That kind of thing only happens now at funerals. The family is very divided and spread out. The Hyannis Port compound thing is fading fast.

"It was a weird occasion," she continued. "In a way, it was to say farewell to Ted. But in Ted's eyes, it was to heal a rift in the family, which was divided over its support for the newly elected president, Barack Obama. Ted, of course, had enthusiastically endorsed Obama during the primary campaign and general election, calling Obama a man with extraordinary gifts of leadership and character. And Caroline [Kennedy] said that Obama offered the same sense of hope and inspiration as her father. But there were naysayers present at Hyannis Port, notably Bobby [Robert Kennedy Jr.], who had been all for Hillary and was still a bitter critic of Obama.

"Ted wanted to convince the family to speak with one voice so that they would have more political power in the future. It was the kind of advice his dad, old Joe Kennedy, would have given. It was a huge thing for Ted, something he was willing to spend his last breath on."

———————

Frail though he was, Ted was eager to take the fight directly to Bobby who, along with his sisters, Kathleen Kennedy Townsend and Kerry Kennedy, led the family faction that had supported Hillary. There had always been tensions at Kennedy

family gatherings—fist fights and overturned tables were not unheard of—and this event was no exception. Bobby told his uncle in no uncertain terms that he deeply resented the outrageous way the Obama people had tried to hang the charge of racism on Bill Clinton. For Bobby, like his father, Robert F. Kennedy, everything was personal; Bobby had two children who suffered from asthma, and he didn't think Obama took environmental issues like air quality seriously enough. Bobby also argued that Obama had no experience and was going to make a complete botch of things.

As he listened to Ted try to defend Obama, Bobby got hot under the collar and started pointing his finger in his uncle's face. He kept saying over and over, "If you don't listen to me, you're going to regret it." When Ted tried to explain his position, Bobby interrupted, saying, "Obama talks about clean coal. There's no such thing as clean coal!" His brothers, Max and Joe, had to intervene and urge him to drop the argument.

During the luncheon, Ted proposed a toast to Obama—not once, but twice. He spoke feelingly, but from a seated position, because he no longer had the strength to stand. Caroline joined her uncle's toast, even though she had developed some early misgivings about Obama's team of advisers. During a recent meeting of Obama's aides at Ted's home in the Kalorama section of Washington, D.C., Caroline had offered several ideas about education reform to Arne Duncan, Obama's secretary of education. Duncan listened politely but seemed unimpressed by Caroline's point of view. She wasn't used to people ignoring her suggestions, and she was still smarting from the experience.

Nonetheless, Caroline offered a few words of praise for Obama. She spoke about how hard she had worked for his election. She said that Obama was serious about ending the wars in Iraq and Afghanistan.

Bobby sat there, fuming. He had always found Caroline too smug for his taste. Her words angered him, and he squeezed his fluted glass so hard that it shattered in his hand, shocking everyone and causing a sudden silence.

———————

Two months later, Ted Kennedy was dead, and for the first time in more than seventy-five years, the clan was without a chieftain. In Ted's place, power was split among three cousins: Joseph P. Kennedy II, a former congressman who ran Citizens Energy Corp., a non-profit oil company; Robert Kennedy Jr., the environmental activist and syndicated talk-show host; and Caroline Kennedy, the most famous and popular living Kennedy of all.

For the most part, Joe Kennedy remained mum about the Obama administration, leaving it to his brother Bobby to make fiery speeches attacking the president for his environmental policies. That left Caroline, who had showered Obama with all her prestige and celebrity. She was the only Kennedy who had reason to expect something in return from Obama, and she didn't waste any time asking for a plum appointment.

Since Caroline's abortive run for the United States Senate from New York, she had lost all interest in elective office. But she wanted to secure a position as an adviser on education to the new

Barack Hussein Obama. According to those who know him best, he represents something new in American politics—the Amateur—a president who is inept in the arts of management and governance and repeats policies that make our economy less robust and our nation less safe. *(Pete Souza/PSG/Newscom)*

Obama campaigning for the Illinois Senate, 1995. "He had no interest in the process, or in learning the process of being a good senator. He just wanted to stand on the Senate floor and give speeches." *(Marc PoKempner)*

The Clintons at a Memorial Day event in Puerto Rico. Bill urged Hillary to think the unthinkable and challenge Obama for their party's presidential nomination in 2012. *(Brennan Linsley/AP Images)*

Obama on the March 2003 cover of *N'DIGO*—a first for the state senator. At the time, his marriage was on the rocks, and Obama confided to friends that he and Michelle were talking about divorce. *(Courtesy of N'DIGO)*

Obama with the Reverend Jesse Jackson Sr. during a Congressional Black Caucus event, 2006. Perhaps out of fear of alienating white voters, Obama never acknowledged his debt to Jackson. *(Tom Williams/RollCall/Polaris)*

ABOVE: Obama and first friend Eric Whitaker exchange a fist bump, 2010. Unbeknownst to the press corps, Whitaker handled some of Obama's stickiest personal problems. *(Alex Brandon/AP Images)*

RIGHT: The Reverend Jeremiah Wright, center, at Chicago's Saint Sabina Catholic Church, 2008. "After the media went ballistic on me," Wright said, "I received an email offering me money not to preach." *(Chris Sweda/Chicago Sun-Times/AP Images)*

Michelle, daughters Malia and Sasha, and Barack Obama with Jesse Jackson at the Rainbow/PUSH Coalition, 2004. Jackson invited Obama to speak at PUSH every Saturday so that he could hone his speaking skills. *(Nam Y. Huh/AP Images)*

U.S. Senate candidate Obama speaks to supporters at the Community Fellowship Baptist Church in Chicago, 2006. "I bring you greetings from my pastor, the Reverend Jeremiah Wright," Obama began his speeches. *(Anne Ryan/Polaris)*

The Reverend Otis Moss, Jeremiah Wright's successor at Trinity United Church of Christ, 2008. Moss told Wright that the Obama campaign was "trying to drive a wedge between us, and I'm not gonna do that." *(M. Spencer Green/AP Images)*

Father Michael Pfleger speaks at the annual Martin Luther King Jr. Commemorative Service, 2003. Pfleger attacked Eric Whitaker from the pulpit of Trinity United Church of Christ. *(Tami Chappell/Reuters)*

Al Capone walks out of Federal Court in Chicago, 1931. Obama is the product of Chicago-style politics, which is a byword for patronage, nepotism, bribery, and corruption. *(AP Images)*

White House Chief of Staff Rahm Emanuel whispers into the president's ear, 2010. Emanuel resented the fact that Michelle Obama sent scolding emails that were passed around the White House, undercutting his authority. *(Charles Dharapak/AP Images)*

LEFT: Obama with his consigliere, Valerie Jarrett, 2010. Trying to figure out Jarrett's mysterious hold on the president and first lady is a favorite guessing game in the parlors and dining rooms of Washington.
(Jason Reed/Reuters)

BELOW: Feuding advisers Rahm Emanuel and Valerie Jarrett listen as the president meets with his economic advisers, 2009. At almost every turn, Emanuel was thwarted by Jarrett.
(Larry Downing/Reuters)

RIGHT: Presidential advisers, from left, David Axelrod, David Plouffe, Robert Gibbs (in the background), and Valerie Jarrett. As charter members of the Cult of Obama, they made certain that the president remained true to his roots as a big-spending, big-government liberal.
(J. Scott Applewhite/AP Images)

BELOW: Obama with Solyndra CEO Chris Gronet, 2010. Before the solar company went bankrupt, National Economic Council director Lawrence Summers warned, "The government is a crappy venture capitalist."
(Alex Brandon/AP Images)

Democratic presidential candidate Obama is joined by Senator Edward Kennedy during a rally at American University, 2008. Practically every major measure proposed during Obama's four years in office flowed from Ted Kennedy's endorsement. *(Jason Reed/Reuters)*

LEFT: First Lady Michelle Obama in the East Room of the White House, 2011. Of all the ways the mainstream media have kowtowed to the Obamas, none has been more disgraceful than their coverage of Barack's marriage to Michelle.
(Patsy Lynch/Polaris)

BELOW: Michelle Obama with her husband and David Axelrod at Invesco Field, Denver, 2008. Their stealth co-presidency has obscured the fact that the Obamas share a sense of entitlement, a contempt for the political process, and a callow understanding of the way the world works.
(Alex Brandon/AP Images)

ABOVE: Michelle Obama with French first lady Carla Bruni-Sarkozy at the Palais Rohan in Strasbourg, France, 2009. Michelle denied telling the French first lady that life in the White House was "hell," but no one believed her. *(Charles Dharapak/AP Images)*

RIGHT: White House social secretary Desirée Rogers on the South Lawn of the White House, 2009. Rogers and Valerie Jarrett resented Oprah Winfrey meddling in their bailiwick. *(Polaris)*

Obama meets Israeli Prime Minister Benjamin
"Bibi" Netanyahu in the Oval Office, 2012. Along
with most Israelis, Netanyahu was shocked and
appalled by Obama's display of rank amateurism
in the art of diplomatic negotiations.
(Pablo Martinez Monsivals/AP Images)

Retired Marine general James Jones speaks at a Chicago news conference in 2008 after being tapped by President-elect Obama to be his National Security Adviser. There were signs from the beginning that Jones' calm, systematic approach to problems did not fit the frenetic, highly politicized atmosphere in the Obama White House. *(John Gress/Reuters)*

National Security Adviser James Jones listens to Obama speak about troop reductions at Camp Lejeune, North Carolina, 2009. Jones described Obama's Chicago aides as the "Politburo" and the "Mafia." His wife called them "a bunch of Chicago thugs." *(Charles Dharapak/ AP Images)*

Obama (back to camera) bows before Saudi Arabia's King Abdullah.
Obama was following the lead of foreign policy adviser Samantha Power,
who advised, "Instituting a policy of mea culpa would enhance
[America's] credibility." *(John Stillwell/AP Images)*

September 11 terrorist mastermind Khalid Sheikh Mohammed. Against the advice of Rahm Emanuel, Obama supported Attorney General Eric Holder's hare-brained scheme to try the terrorist in a civilian court not far from the ruins of the World Trade Center. *(AP Images)*

Secretary of State Hillary Rodham Clinton, President Barack Obama, and Vice President Joe Biden, along with members of the national security team, receive an update on the mission against Osama bin Laden in the Situation Room of the White House in Washington. *(Pete Souza/The White House/AP Images)*

administration. With that in mind, she sent the White House a long memo on education funding reform, which was based on her first-hand experience with the New York City Board of Education. She ended the memo by saying that she hoped to meet with the president to discuss her ideas.

She never got a response. Not even an acknowledgement that he had received the memo.

Then, in the summer of 2011, Caroline asked Maurice Tempelsman, her mother's longtime companion and a major player in the Democratic Party, to arrange a meeting with the president and his political advisers on Tempelsman's 70-foot yacht the *Relemar*, which was docked on Martha's Vineyard, where the president was vacationing. It was Caroline's hope that such a meeting would further her late Uncle Teddy's dream of forming a close bond between the Kennedys and the Obamas.

Once again, the White House spurned Caroline's overture. The president didn't even make an effort to see Caroline, whose home on Martha's Vineyard, Red Gate Farm, was not far from the house the president was renting. A presidential snub had turned into an insult.

The White House meted out similar treatment to Ethel Kennedy, the matriarch of the family. During the presidential primaries and general election, Ethel was so gung-ho for Obama that she stopped talking to her son Bobby, because he was an Obama critic. After Obama won the election, Ethel invited the new president to stop by her house in the Kennedy Compound. Her request was met with stony silence. Ethel was so angry that she went on a rampage inside her house, cursing the president and turning over furniture.

"Our family has spies all over the Obama administration," said a member of the Kennedy clan. "There are a lot of Kennedy loyalists from Ted's old office and his connections throughout Washington who are in high positions in the White House agencies. People like Melody Barnes, the director of the Domestic Policy Council; Kenneth Feinberg, the special master of the September 11th Victim Compensation Fund; James Steinberg, a former deputy secretary of state; and Greg Craig, the former White House counsel under Obama.

"Through these and other people, Caroline heard back that there was a lot of nasty shit being said about the Kennedys by the president and Michelle," the family member continued. "There were catty remarks about how badly the Kennedy women dressed, and how their houses were shabby and threadbare. Caroline got the impression that most of this negativity was coming from Michelle, who didn't want the Kennedys to be part of the administration for fear that they would have too much influence over the president.

"Gradually, Caroline began to change her tune and side with Bobby and Kathleen [Kennedy Townsend] against the Obamas. Unlike Jackie, who was completely a-political, Caroline is liberal with a capital L. When Obama didn't raise taxes to balance the budget, Caroline marked him down. In her eyes, he's a mess because he doesn't follow the liberal bible on politics. More important, Caroline discovered that the Obamas didn't give a damn about her or her support. For instance, she was not invited to the state dinners at the White House hosted by the Obamas, or to the president's forty-ninth birthday celebration in Chicago.

"It really annoyed Caroline when comparisons were made by the media between Michelle and Jackie. Caroline had a word for such comparisons; she called them 'odious.' She really got annoyed. And when she began to fall out of love with the Obamas, love was replaced by outright scorn. Now she says things about Obama like, 'I can't stand to hear his voice any more. He's a liar and worse.'"

———————

On Halloween, 2011, Caroline Kennedy received an invitation to attend a reception celebrating the fiftieth anniversary of the White House Historical Society. She could hardly have been ignored in this case because it was her mother, Jacqueline Bouvier Kennedy, who had restored many parts of the White House and established the White House Historical Association in 1961.

The reception was closed to the press. Michelle Obama posed for a photo with Caroline, which was released later. But that was it. There was no invitation to the Family Quarters, where Caroline had lived and played as a child. After the photo, Michelle spun on her heels and left.

"Caroline said that shaking hands with Michelle was like shaking hands with a cold fish," a close family adviser who talked with Caroline after the White House event said. "Caroline had the feeling she wasn't really wanted there. Michelle gave the distinct impression that she doesn't like her. Caroline can be pretty standoffish herself, but she was surprised at how cold Michelle was to her.

"The only thing personal about the meeting was when Michelle turned to Caroline and said, 'The president is going to put the Keystone Pipeline project on hold and wouldn't Bobby like that?' In response, Caroline said, 'Bobby would like to meet with the president about the Keystone Pipeline being not only delayed, but being aggressively attacked and killed.' Michelle looked stricken. She said, 'Bobby should call the White House,' meaning that he would have to go through channels like everybody else.

"Caroline's attitude about the 2012 election is that, as a loyal Democrat, she has nowhere to go, no one else to possibly support except Obama. What really pisses her off is that the Obamas know that she has nowhere else to go, so they see no point in being nice to her."

CHAPTER 15

THE JEWISH PROBLEM WITH OBAMA

*Jews earn like Episcopalians and
vote like Puerto Ricans.*

—Milton Himmelfarb

Nothing pleased Barack Obama more than the opportunity to leave his carping critics behind and escape overseas, where his reputation as an amateur had not caught up with him. And so last November, after bashing the Republicans for failing to pass an expensive jobs bill that he knew in advance would never collect the necessary votes, the embattled president eagerly bounded up the ramp of Air Force One for the nine-hour flight to Cannes, in the south of France, where he was scheduled to rub shoulders with presidents, prime ministers, and heads of state at the Group of 20 summit meeting.

Three thousand five hundred journalists and a fleet of two hundred motorcycle escorts were on hand to greet Obama. The city center was locked down by twelve thousand security guards and ten thousand metal barriers. Snipers were positioned on top of hotels and all the high points in the city, and divers inspected the port and its boats. Yachts were forbidden to dock off Cannes' famous Boulevard de la Croisette. The Palais des Festivals, which hosts the annual Cannes Film Festival, was booked to accommodate the visiting dignitaries. Photos of Obama mingling with his fellow summiteers and looking like the Leader of the Free World were transmitted back to the United States, where Obama's handlers hoped they would man-up his wussy image.

For Obama, the spectacle in Cannes recalled the heady days during the 2008 presidential campaign when he was treated like the Second Coming of the Messiah. As he relaxed among friends in the French resort city, years of care seemed to melt from the lines on his face. By the time he sat down with his host, the president of France, Nicolas Sarkozy, for a private conversation before a final press conference, Obama was in such a relaxed and jovial mood that he didn't notice the open microphone nearby. His subsequent conversation was recorded by reporters in an adjoining room.

"Netanyahu!" said Sarkozy, referring to Israeli Prime Minister Benjamin "Bibi" Netanyahu. "I can't stand him. He's a liar."

To which an unguarded American president replied: "*You're* sick of him? I have to work with him every day."

The publication of Obama's impolitic comment, first reported · by a French website and confirmed by the Associated Press, provided a window into the president's true feelings about Bibi Netanyahu and his right-of-center government in Israel. Obama entered office with the professed goal of bringing about an independent Palestinian state before the end of his first term, and he blamed Netanyahu, rather than his own misguided policies and the pitfalls of the Israeli-Palestinian dispute, for preventing him from reaching that objective.

Just six months before the Cannes summit, Obama had set off a firestorm in Israel by calling upon the Jewish state to accept its 1967 borders, with agreed upon land swamps, as a basis for resuming negotiations with the Palestinians. Along with most Israelis, Netanyahu was shocked and appalled by Obama's display of rank amateurism in the art of diplomatic negotiations. Like previous Israeli prime ministers, Netanyahu was prepared to negotiate on the basis of the 1967 borders, but he wasn't so naïve that he would give away that key negotiating point without demanding that the Palestinians first agree to recognize the legitimacy of the state of Israel. As a result, Netanyahu rejected Obama's initiative, handing the American president yet another foreign policy setback, and sinking relations between Washington and Jerusalem to their lowest point since the administration of Jimmy Carter.

This, in turn, had serious domestic consequences for Obama's relations with one of his key political constituencies—the

American Jewish community. "Jewish voters," wrote Erica Werner of the Associated Press, "though comprising only 2 percent of the electorate nationwide, are an important part of Obama's base and could make a difference in battleground states including Florida, Pennsylvania, Ohio, and Nevada in a close election. Moreover, the Jewish community is an important source of donations, and Obama campaign supporters want to maintain that support as much as Republicans want to chip away at it."

In the nearly eighty years since President Franklin Roosevelt's New Deal, relations between American Jews and the Democratic Party had been as close as lips and teeth. Even as Jews prospered and assimilated into the mainstream of American life, most of them remained loyal to FDR's liberal vision and refrained from following the pattern of other affluent groups by shifting to the Republican Party. Over the course of the past twenty presidential election cycles, a stunning 75 percent of the Jewish vote has on average gone to the Democratic presidential candidate.

If further proof of Jewish loyalty to the Democrats were needed, it was provided by the 2008 election of Barack Obama. On a key issue for many Jewish voters—support for Israel—the hawkish John McCain started off with a decisive advantage over Obama, whose past associations with the anti-Semitic Reverend Jeremiah Wright and the Israel-bashing Columbia University Professor Rashid Khalidi raised troubling questions in the minds of many Jews. And yet, when the vote was tallied, Obama trounced McCain among Jews by a staggering 57-point margin.

"After decades of involvement in the civil rights movement by American Jews, Obama stirred deep emotions in the Jewish community," Bret Stephens, the deputy editorial page editor of the *Wall Street Journal*, told the author of this book. "The black-Jewish alliance was shattered in the late 1960s, and Jews have yearned ever since to restore it. Jews felt good about voting for Obama, for not only were they voting for a guy they agreed with and liked, but they were also voting for their own personal redemption."

A sizable number of American Jews, however, are having a serious case of buyer's remorse when it comes to Barack Obama. Recent polls of the Jewish community reflect a significant decline in support from 2008, when 78 percent of Jewish voters pulled the lever for Obama. According to one poll, Obama's approval rating among American Jews has plummeted to 54 percent. Others, such as a survey of the American Jewish Committee, have cast it even lower.

Among the many factors driving down Obama's numbers among Jewish voters was the president's hostile attitude toward businessmen in general and Wall Street in particular. But what really appeared to irritate American Jews was the president's roughhouse treatment of Israel.

As the 2012 presidential election drew near, Obama backed off from some of his public assaults on Israel, and hired a high-level Jewish outreach director to smooth over hurt feelings. But Obama was still in trouble with large segments of the Jewish community. The 2011 annual survey by the American Jewish Committee revealed declining Jewish support for Obama. Among its findings:

- For the first time during Obama's presidency, disapproval among Jewish voters exceeded approval by 48 to 45 percent
- Obama's approval rating among Jews had dropped 10 percent in the past twelve months
- A majority (53 percent) disapproved of Obama's handling of Israel-U.S. relations
- A plurality of Jews (45 percent) disapproved of Obama's handling of the Iran nuclear issue
- A majority (55 percent) opposed establishing a Palestinian state "in the current situation"

Malcolm Hoenlein, co-chairman of the Conference of Presidents of Major American Jewish Organizations, the coordinating body for fifty-two Jewish groups, estimated that Obama had lost the support of as much as one-third of Jewish voters. Sid Dinerstein, chairman of the Palm Beach County Republican Party, predicted that Obama would be limited to around 60 percent of the Jewish vote in 2012. While these estimates are just that, predictions, there is no denying the fact that many Jews are so annoyed with the Obama administration that they have closed their wallets and are seriously thinking of sitting out the 2012 election.

"President Barack Obama's Chicago-based reelection campaign has a hometown problem: the donors and volunteers who have lost interest after launching his run for the White House four years ago," Steven R. Strahler and Paul Merrion wrote in September 2011 in ChicagoBusiness.com. "And among Jewish contributors, a bulwark of his local donor base, some have been turned off by Mr. Obama's call for Israel to give up part of its territory."

"The assumption on the part of the Obama administration is that because Jews are liberals, they simply will not vote for Republicans," said the Hollywood billionaire Haim Saban, one of the Democratic Party's mega-donors. "Obama can invite the ten most prolific Jewish campaign bundlers to the White House for a discussion, and give a wonderful speech, and he'll think that this may resolve all his problems with American Jews. And it may—or it may not."

"The idea that we saw a black president in our lifetime is wonderful," said New York City's former mayor, Ed Koch. "It conveyed to us that this country has come such a long way. But I never fully accepted that Obama didn't hear his minister [Jeremiah Wright] make those awful anti-Semitic statements over twenty years. I wanted to believe him. I willed myself to believe him.... What he has done is break that trust. Like Humpty Dumpty, once you break it, you can't put it together again."

The Jewish problem with Obama could be traced back to his first full day on the job. On January 21, 2009, he summoned his national security team to the Oval Office and laid out a tough new policy toward Israel. Obama said that in order to make good on his campaign promise to extricate 200,000 American troops from the wars in Iraq and Afghanistan, the U.S. had to create a grand coalition of "moderate" Muslim states and Israel to isolate

Iran, which had made no secret of its ambition to become the nuclear hegemon in the Middle East.

The only way to accomplish that goal, the president stated, was to eliminate the poisonous effect of the Israeli-Palestinian conflict, which provided Iran with an excuse to stir up trouble. Thus it was "a vital national interest of the United States" to stop Israel from building settlements in the occupied West Bank and housing in East Jerusalem, and *force* the Jewish state to resolve the Palestinian problem.

Previous White Houses had made similar noises about bringing peace to the Middle East, and at first Jewish leaders didn't pay much attention to leaks emanating from the new administration about a fundamental change in American policy. However, a clue to the president's true intentions came in March 2009, when Abe Foxman, the national director of the Anti-Defamation League, met with the president's then chief of staff, Rahm Emanuel.

"This is Israel's moment of truth," Emanuel told Foxman. "This President is determined to make peace between Israel and the Arabs."

To many Jews, it seemed highly improbable that a brand new president would choose to alienate Israel, America's oldest and most loyal ally in the Middle East. But then, in July 2009, when President Obama made his first overseas trip, he chose to visit three Muslim countries—Turkey, Saudi Arabia, and Egypt. During a landmark speech in Cairo, he announced his intention to seek "a new beginning between the United States and Muslims around the world."

Understandably enough, American Jews were annoyed that the president had failed to include Israel in his Mideast swing.

But what rankled them even more was that Obama seemed to adopt the Arab narrative to explain the existence of Israel—namely, that Israel was created because of past Jewish suffering in Europe, particularly during the Holocaust. Nowhere in his Cairo speech did Obama mention the fact that Jews had a 3,000-year history in the Promised Land.

Things went from bad to worse when the president called a meeting of Jewish leaders in July. Fourteen major Jewish organizations were represented at this meeting, including J Street, the newly formed left-of-center Jewish lobby. J Street is on the same wavelength as the Peace Now movement in Israel, which believes that continued occupation of the West Bank harms Israel both economically and politically and damages the values and fabric of the Jewish state.

Rabbi Eric Joffe, a Reform Jewish leader, asked the president why he had singled out Israel for public criticism.

"Look," said the thin-skinned president, clearly annoyed by the question, "we have some very smart people on this. Don't think that we don't understand the nuances of the settlement issue. We do. Rahm [Emanuel] understands the politics there, and he explains them to me."

Some of the Jews attending the meeting were shocked to hear the president admit that he had to be educated about Israel's concerns.

"I agree with your goal to bring peace to the Middle East," the Anti-Defamation League's Abe Foxman told the president. "But the perception is that you're beating up only on Israel, and not on the Arabs. If you want Israel to take risks for peace, the best way is to make Israel feel that its staunch friend America is behind it."

"You are absolutely wrong," the president replied. "For the past eight years [under the Bush administration], Israel had a friend in the United States and it didn't make peace."

"I came away from the meeting convinced that Obama has introduced a new and dangerous strategy and that it's revealing itself in steps," Foxman told me. "Unlike other administrations, this one is applying linkage in the Middle East. It's saying that if you resolve the Israeli-Palestinian conflict, the messiah will come and the lions will lie down with the lambs. All the president's advisers on the Middle East, starting with George Mitchell, believe in linkage, and they're telling the president you have to prove to the Arab Muslim world that you are different than previous presidents and you can separate yourself from Israel, distance yourself from the settlements issue. After all, settlements are something that American Jews don't like anyway, so it's a win-win proposition."

The Anti-Defamation League was the first mainstream Jewish organization to openly criticize the president on the issue of the Middle East. Soon, other groups began to join the chorus. However, the great majority of Jews still remained steadfast behind Obama and his administration's liberal agenda. They simply were not ready to criticize their country's first African-American president, a man in whom they had invested so many of their own hopes and dreams.

On March 10, 2010, a relatively low-level official in the Israeli Interior Ministry issued a permit for 1,600 new housing units for Israelis in the Ramat Shlomo section of East Jerusalem. The ill-timed announcement came on the very day Vice President Joe Biden arrived in Israel to kick-start a round of indirect peace talks between Israel and the Palestinians. Israeli Prime Minister Benjamin Netanyahu immediately apologized to Biden, who accepted his expression of regret. But Mahmoud Abbas, president of the Palestinian National Authority on the West Bank, called off the "proximity talks."

The next day, at the regularly scheduled weekly breakfast meeting between the president and Secretary of State Hillary Clinton, Obama made his feelings clear. He was livid. As he saw it, the Israelis had purposely humiliated his vice president and tried to sabotage his peace plan. It was a personal affront, and he wouldn't stand for such treatment. He instructed Hillary to call Netanyahu and read him the riot act.

The following day, during a 43-minute harangue, Hillary delivered a set of ultimatums to Netanyahu. Prefacing each remark with the phrase "I have been instructed to tell you," Hillary demanded that Israel release a substantial number of Palestinian prisoners as a token of goodwill; lift its siege of Gaza; suspend all settlements in the West Bank and Jerusalem; accept that a symbolic number of Palestinians be given the "right of return" to Israel under a future peace treaty; and agree to place the question of the status of Jerusalem at the top of the peace-talks agenda.

"If you refuse these demands," Hillary told Netanyahu, "the United States government will conclude that we no longer share the same interests."

Netanyahu bit his tongue and remained noncommittal about the American demands, though he did eventually agree to ease the blockade of Gaza.

That same Friday, the Israeli ambassador to Washington, Michael Oren, was summoned to the State Department and given a severe dressing down. Someone who saw Oren that night at a party described him as "shaken."

And things did not end there. Ten days later, Netanyahu was invited to the White House, where he was treated to further browbeating and humiliation. Photographers were banned from recording the visit. And at one point, President Obama left Netanyahu to have dinner with Michelle and their daughters, Malia and Sasha.

"I'm going upstairs," the president told Netanyahu. "Call me when you're ready to talk substance."

Netanyahu and his entourage were then left to cool their heels in the Roosevelt Room. At one point, the Israeli delegation asked for food and something to drink. They were served non-kosher food, which some of them couldn't eat.

The White House seemed strangely indifferent to the feelings of resentment that its treatment of Netanyahu aroused in the Jewish community. For shortly after Netanyahu returned to Israel, President Obama risked provoking even greater Jewish outrage by insinuating that American troops were dying in Iraq and Afghanistan because Israel refused to agree to peace with the Palestinians. The Israeli-Arab conflict "is costing us significantly in terms of both blood and treasure," the president said.

A perception began to spread throughout the Jewish community that the Obama administration was not only outwardly hostile to Israel, but perhaps, without even knowing it, hostile to Jews as well. This thesis was forcefully argued by Jonathan Kellerman, bestselling novelist and a professor of clinical pediatrics and psychology at the University of Southern California's Keck School of Medicine:

> My personal opinion... is that the bifurcation of Israel and Judaism is structurally fallacious. The Land of Israel is an essential ingredient of Judaism practiced fully. Thus, it is impossible to be anti-Israel and not be anti-Jewish. And in fact, the war being waged against Israel by the Muslim world is, at the core, a religious dispute. Radical Islamists no longer talk about Zionists; they come right out and broadcast their goal of eradicating worldwide Jewry.

The impression of an anti-Jewish bias at the highest echelons of the Obama administration, though unproved, was given added force in April when James Jones, the retired Marine Corps four-star general who then served as President Obama's national security adviser, delivered a speech at the Washington Institute for Near East Policy. He opened his remarks with a joke that was widely interpreted by many Jews as being flagrantly anti-Semitic. Said Jones:

> I'd just like to tell you a story that I think is true. It happened recently in southern Afghanistan. A member of the Taliban was separated from his fighting party and wandered around for a few days in the desert, lost, out of food, no water. And he looked on the horizon and he saw what looked like a little shack and he walked towards that shack. And as he got to it, it

turned out it was a little store owned by a Jewish merchant. And the Taliban warrior went up to him and said, "I need water. Give me some water." And the merchant said, "I'm sorry, I don't have any water, but would you like a tie? We have a nice sale of ties today."

Whereupon the Taliban erupted into a stream of language that I can't repeat, but about Israel, about Jewish people, about the man himself, about his family, and just said, "I need water, you try to sell me ties, you people don't get it."

And impassively the merchant stood there until the Taliban was through with his diatribe and said, "Well I'm sorry that I don't have water for you and I forgive you for all of the insults you've levied against me, my family, my country. But I will help you out. If you go over that hill and walk about two miles, there is a restaurant there and they have all the water you need." And the Taliban, instead of saying thanks, still muttering under his breath, disappears over the hill, only to come back an hour later. And walking up to the merchant says, "Your brother tells me [you] need a tie to get into the restaurant."

———

At a certain point, many Jews began to wonder if there was something more behind the Obama administration's confrontational approach toward Israel than a simple difference of policy. As a result, they began to take a second look at Obama's past for clues to his present behavior. In particular, they were curious how Chicago's bare-knuckle politics had shaped Obama's outlook.

"Maybe Jews and blacks were once the closest of allies in Chicago," said Joseph Aaron, the liberal editor of *The Jewish News*, Chicago's largest Jewish newspaper. "But in the years that Obama was being shaped, a lot of young blacks, especially in the South Side neighborhood where Obama lived, harbored animosity toward Jews and Israel.

"Two central issues divided blacks and Jews in those years," Aaron continued. "Blacks saw affirmative action as a way to overcome prejudice, while many Jews saw it as a quota system designed to keep them out. It was also a time when Israel, snubbed by many nations, especially in black Africa, chose to forge close ties with the apartheid regime in South Africa. That included selling Israeli arms to South Africa. We never realized the degree to which those links to South Africa hurt black sensitivities.

"Add it all up and you don't come up with an anti-Semitic Obama. That is not who Obama is. What you do come up with is someone who doesn't really understand our attachment to Israel or Israel's importance to Jews as a people, a president who doesn't have a gut love for Israel like some of his predecessors, but someone who understands the Palestinian position better than any president we've had, someone with no natural affinity for Jews or Israel, and someone who approaches the Middle East, as he does most everything else, dispassionately and with a burning desire to fix the problem."

As the *New York Times* wrote about Obama in the months leading up to the 2008 Democratic National Convention:

The secret of his transformation [from a newcomer] to the brink of claiming the Democratic presidential nomination can be described as the politics of maximum unity. [Obama] moved from his leftist... base to more centrist circles; he forged early alliances with the good-government reform crowd only to be embraced later by the city's all-powerful Democratic bosses; he railed against pork-barrel politics but engaged in it when needed; and he empathized with the views of the Palestinian friends before adroitly courting the city's politically potent Jewish community.

That courtship brought Obama the support of some of the wealthiest Jews in Chicago. They included Penny Pritzker of the Hyatt Hotel chain family; Betty Lu Saltzman, daughter of the late real-estate baron Philip Klutznick; former Congressman Abner Mikva; Lester Crown, a billionaire benefactor of Jewish charities; and Lee Rosenberg, a media and entertainment mogul, who accompanied Obama on his 2004 senatorial election campaign visit to Israel, where Obama placed a handwritten prayer for peace in the cracks of Jerusalem's Western Wall.

Few of these early Jewish sponsors have since publicly criticized the president for his tough line on Israel. But at least three of his Chicago backers—Penny Pritzker, Lester Crown, and Lee Rosenberg, the president of the powerful pro-Israel lobby AIPAC (America-Israel Public Affairs Committee)—expressed their distress in private conversations with Obama.

Some people blamed Obama's Jewish problem on his advisers, including his former chief of staff Rahm Emanuel, whose Israeli father was a member of the Irgun underground during Israel's struggle for independence, and Valerie Jarrett, who made no secret of her close ties to the Jordanian royal family. But veteran journalist Richard Z. Chesnoff, who has had more than forty years of experience reporting from the Middle East, and who's done extensive research on Obama's management style, didn't agree with that assessment.

"In my opinion," said Chesnoff, "Obama's problem in dealing with the Arab-Israeli conundrum doesn't come from the advice he's getting from his advisers, but rather from his one-man style and his inflated view of his own leadership talents. Obama believes that no matter what the odds against it, he can bring everyone together, kumbaya style, so that we can solve hitherto insoluble problems. Perhaps even more egregiously, he seems to have an exaggerated sense of his own depth of understanding of the Middle East, which is simply not borne out by his background or experience."

"The problem is naïveté in the Obama administration," added Robert Lieber, professor of government at Georgetown University. "The president came into office with the assumption that the Israel-Palestinian conflict is by far the most central urgent problem in the region—which it is not—and that it is the key that unlocks everything else in the region. And he and his advisers believed the [Israeli-Palestinian] situation was ripe for progress, which it absolutely isn't."

By the end of March 2010, most of the organized Jewish community was in full cry against the Obama administration's treatment of Israel. However, the voice of New York's senior senator, Chuck Schumer, one of the most influential elected Jewish officials in Washington, was conspicuously silent. That gave Ed Koch, an incurable gadfly, the opportunity to taunt his frenemy Schumer in his blog, "Ed Koch Commentary."

"Chuck Schumer resented my blog," Koch told me. "He called me and said, 'How can you say this? I'm a protector of Israel.' And I said, 'Chuck, you're not speaking out!' And he said, 'I'm doing it behind the scenes.' He was upset because there was a piece quoting me as saying, 'It's obvious Chuck wants to be the majority leader in the Senate if Harry Reid leaves, and Chuck doesn't want to criticize the president and diminish his chances.'"

Throughout April 2010, the pressure on Schumer continued to mount. Finally, when P. J. Crowley, the State Department spokesman, announced at a press conference that the relationship of Israel and the United States depended on the pace of peace negotiations, Schumer could no longer hold his tongue.

"This is terrible," Schumer said. "That is a dagger, because the relationship is much deeper than the disagreements on negotiations, and most Americans—Democrat, Republican, Jew, non-Jew—would feel that. So I called up Rahm Emanuel and I called up the White House and I said, 'If you don't retract that statement, you are going to hear me publicly blast you on this.'

"You have to show Israel that it's not going to be forced to do things it doesn't want to do and can't do," Schumer continued. "At the same time, you have to show the Palestinians that they are not going to get their way by just sitting back and not giving in, and not recognizing that there is a state of Israel. And right now, there is a battle going on inside the administration. One side agrees with us, one side doesn't, and we're pushing hard to make sure the right side wins and, if not, we'll have to take it to the next step."

After Schumer's J'accuse, it became clear that the inexperienced Obama had once again overplayed his hand. In part, the president had allowed himself to be influenced by the growing volume of anti-Israel anger coming from the left wing of the Democratic Party, especially from radical students on campuses, where calls for the "delegitimization" of the Jewish State were almost *de rigueur*. In part, too, the president probably placed too much weight on recent sociological studies that indicated a shift in American Jewish attitudes on Israel.

In May 2010, under mounting pressure, the president agreed to meet with Jewish members of the Democratic caucuses in the House and Senate. Thirty-seven of the forty-three Jews in Congress met with Obama, the largest such gathering of Jewish lawmakers ever held in the White House. One of the attendees, who took notes during the meeting, made them available to the author of this book. Here is a transcript of what Obama said to the Jewish congressmen and women:

> [Palestinian Prime Minister Salam] Fayyad and Abu Mazen [Palestinian Liberation Organization chairman Mahmoud Abbas] are as moderate as we are going to get.

My policy on settlements is no different than George Bush's, but I won't wink or nod.

You want me to be explicit on Iran, but as the guy with his finger on the button, I am not going to say anything. When I say [an Iranian nuclear weapon is] unacceptable, it's unacceptable.

Bibi's speech at AIPAC [the American Israel Public Affairs Committee] on Jerusalem was belligerent.

I'm pro-Israel not pro-Shas [an ultra-orthodox religious political party in Israel that opposes any freeze on Israeli settlements in the West Bank].

My job is to protect the national security of the United States.

I fundamentally believe the key to the Middle East is being an evenhanded broker.

I'm pained that people don't think I support Israel. I take responsibility for stubbing my toe on messaging. My views are distorted.

I feel close to the Jewish community. I wouldn't be here without many of you.

There are legitimate differences between the United States and Israel and [between] me and Prime Minister [Netanyahu]. I've spent more time with him than any other foreign leader.

Everyone knows two states is the only solution.

I can't impose a settlement but I may outline a solution for the parties.

> Our public disagreement with Israel gives us cred-
> ibility with the Arab states and compels them to act.

What most disturbed the Jewish members of Congress was that last comment by Obama—namely, that by haranguing Israel in public and portraying it as a villain in the peace process, Washington gained credibility and influence with the Arabs. No one in the room believed that to be true. Quite the opposite, they believed that the bad blood between the Obama administration and Israel encouraged the Arabs to be more, not less, intransigent.

Indeed, after the meeting, Representative Jan Schakowsky of Illinois, one of Obama's most loyal backers, shook her head and admitted: "He doesn't understand that ally-to-ally differences should not be aired in public. He's isolating Israel and putting Israel in a weakened position."

When word of Obama's views inevitably spread beyond the Capital Beltway, it sent shockwaves through the Jewish community. Said one prominent Jewish leader: "You can draw a straight line between that meeting and Obama's fundraising problems with Jews today."

"The majority of today's American Jews don't see themselves as outsiders or victims anymore," said Binyamin Jolkovsky, the publisher and editor of the widely read Internet magazine

JewishWorldReview.com. "That's positive. But that feeling of equality has also produced a communal negative. The fear that came with being an outsider also gave most Jews, even non-religious ones, a cohesive sense of responsibility regarding their Jewish identity in general and Israel in particular.

"That's changed," Jolkovsky continued. "I'm no senior citizen, but today's generation didn't witness the Holocaust, they don't understand what was entailed in the birth of Israel, they don't even remember the real threats of the 1967 Six Day War, they probably never read the novel *Exodus*. The majority of young American Jews think that somehow Israel will always be there. They don't understand that when your enemies say they want to destroy you, they mean it."

Most of all, what Obama didn't count on was that, for all the changes taking place among younger "progressive" Jews, Jerusalem remained a third rail in American politics. The person who seemed to understand that better than anyone else was Elie Wiesel, the Nobel Laureate and Holocaust survivor, who took out full-page ads in April 2010 in major American newspapers to express his views on the city of Jerusalem.

"For me, the Jew that I am, Jerusalem is above politics," Weisel wrote.

> It is mentioned more than six hundred times in Scripture—and not a single time in the Koran. Its presence in Jewish history is overwhelming. There is no more moving prayer in Jewish history than the one expressing our yearning to return to Jerusalem. To many theologians, it IS Jewish history, to many poets, a source of

inspiration. It belongs to the Jewish people and is much more than a city; it is what binds one Jew to another in a way that remains hard to explain. When a Jew visits Jerusalem for the first time, it is not the first time; it is a homecoming.

I interviewed Weisel following a private lunch that he had in early May with President Obama at the White House. "The invitation came before my public statements on Jerusalem," Weisel said. "It was a very good lunch. No small talk. Everything was substance. I understood his position. We didn't agree on everything. The president wanted to know why Bibi [Prime Minister Benjamin Netanyahu] didn't fire the minister who made that Jerusalem announcement [about expanding Jewish housing during Vice President Joe Biden's visit]. I said he would have had to go to his party and say, 'Give me anyone else.' But he didn't and then there was a chain reaction.

"Most of the problems [between America and Israel] remain, but the intensity on both sides and the recriminations are gone," Weisel added. "During our lunch, it was clear that the President does at least know that Jerusalem is the center of Jewish history, and he knows you can't ignore 3,000 to 4,000 years of history. I believe the only way to attain peace is to put Jerusalem at the end of the negotiations, not at the beginning."

Since the shellacking it suffered in the 2010 midterm elections, the Obama administration has softened some of its more controversial Mideast policy initiatives. For instance, on Jerusalem, the White House conceded that the question of the city's status should come at the end of negotiations between Israel and the

Palestinians, as Elie Weisel desired, rather than at the beginning, as the president originally wanted.

Along with this apparent U-turn in substance, the White House launched a charm offensive to win back the allegiance of the Jewish community. The president set the tone. He sent a personal letter to Alan Solow, the former chairman of the Conference of Presidents of Major Jewish Organizations, in which he reasserted his support for Israel's security. And he followed that up with a warm message of greeting on the occasion of Israel's sixty-second independence day.

Meanwhile, pro-Obama rabbis from local communities all over America were invited to the White House for schmooze fests with Rahm Emanuel, Daniel Shapiro, the deputy national security adviser who dealt with the Middle East, and Dennis Ross, the White House's top Iran policy official.

"The three men told the Democratic rabbis that the administration has three priorities in the Middle East," Caroline Glick reported in *The Jerusalem Post*. "First Obama seeks to isolate Iran. Second, he seeks to significantly reduce the U.S. military presence in the Middle East, particularly in Iraq. And third, he seeks to resolve the Palestinian conflict with Israel."

As part of its PR campaign, the White House had David Axelrod do a limited *mea culpa*. "With some of the leadership of the Jewish community there's been some bumps in the road over the past fifteen months," Axelrod admitted in a phone conversation with the author of this book. "Some of those bumps resulted purely from a lack of communication on our part. I don't think we've done as good a job as we could have in our communications with the Jewish community during the first year or so of the administration. We've had a sustained and vigorous round of communications in the last few months, and I think that's been helpful."

The crowning moment in Washington's charm offensive came in July 2010, when Prime Minister Netanyahu returned to Washington and this time was given the red-carpet treatment. He was honored with a working lunch in the Cabinet Room and a photo op with Obama in the Oval Office. But things didn't work out as the White House had planned. As the TV cameras recorded the scene, Netanyahu wagged his finger under Obama's nose and lectured the president on the Middle East. Obama sat there, saying nothing and looking like a weak, immature schoolboy.

But neither the White House's charm offensive nor the minor adjustments it has made in its policies can obscure an irrefutable fact: the changes are tactical and tonal, not substantive. The goal is still the same—to conclude successful peace talks by applying pressure on Israel.

"In my view, the Obama administration has not pulled back from its desire to ingratiate itself with the Arab world," * said Kenneth J. Bialkin, chairman of the American-Israel Friendship League. "Yes, they've pulled back from saying that Israel's

---

* According to CNN, the White House's efforts to ingratiate itself with the Arab world not have worked. Opinion polls indicate that the favorability rating of the United States in much of the Arab world is lower under President Obama than it was during the Bush administration.

conduct endangers the lives of American soldiers in the Middle East. But most of its charm offensive was aimed at damage control."

Domestic politics surely played a role in the president's calculations vis-à-vis the American Jewish community. But Obama was also influenced by his major foreign policy conundrum: how to contain a resurgent Iran. In pursuit of that goal, Obama expected Israel to strike a peace accord with the Palestinians and their Arab allies—no matter how real or unreal that expectation might be.

"Obama and his people believe the Palestinian leadership is genuinely ready for historic compromise," says David Horovitz, the London-born former editor of *The Jerusalem Post*. "The unfortunate consensus in Israel—and not just the hawks—is that while we wish [the Arabs] were [ready], they aren't.... [To] our great sorrow—and to our great cost—we are not convinced that even the relative moderates like Abbas and Prime Minister Fayyad have internalized the idea that Jews have historic rights here too."

Indeed, in the days just before a new round of peace talks began, Palestinian leaders went out of their way to declare that while they might be prepared to negotiate with Israel, they would never recognize the legitimacy of a Jewish state in the Middle East. In other words, nothing fundamental has changed in the Arab approach to Israel's right to exist since the creation of the State of Israel sixty-two years ago.

In March 2012, with the threat of a nuclear war with Iran hanging over both Israel and the United States, Netanyahu was invited back to the White House for yet another face-to-face with

Obama. It was, said Jonathan S. Tobin on the "Contentions" website of *Commentary* magazine in February 2012,

> impossible to ignore the political implications of this summit. With evidence mounting that Obama and the Democrats have been bleeding Jewish support in the last year, the visit [took] the president's charm offensive aimed at convincing the Jewish community he is Israel's best friend to a new level. Netanyahu [had] good reason to play along with Obama's pretense, as he may have to go on dealing with him until January 2017. But the question remained whether the two men [could] sufficiently paper over their personal hostility and policy differences in order for the visit to have the effect the president's political handlers are aiming for.

CHAPTER 16

ALL IN THE FAMILY

This president runs from race like
a black man runs from a cop.

—Michael Eric Dyson, an African-American professor
of sociology at Georgetown University

D uring the months I spent researching and writing this book, I was frequently asked the same question: What surprised you the most about Barack Obama? My answer was always the same. I said that I was surprised by how badly America's first black president had bungled his relations with black America.

"Early on in his presidency," wrote Randall Kennedy in *The Persistence of the Color Line*, "Obama was pressed by some activists and politicians to offer race-specific policies to address the disproportionately high rates of unemployment that have long plagued black and other racial-minority communities. He steadfastly refused to do so.... 'I can't pass laws that say I'm just helping black folks,' he responded when asked about Congressional Black Caucus (CBC) criticism of his employment policy. 'I'm the president of the United States. What I can do is make sure that I am passing laws that help all people, particularly those that are most vulnerable and most in need. That in turn is going to help lift up the African American community.'

"Here Obama was engaging in the old trick of creating a straw man to knock down," Kennedy continued. "The CBC was not requesting policy aimed at 'just helping black folks.' It was requesting policy that would be intended to assist Americans as a whole but 'particularly those who are most vulnerable' in economic downturns.... "

Despite Obama's failed economic policies, grievances between black leaders and the black president were kept under wraps for quite some time. White Americans were hardly aware of the family squabble. But those grievances finally surfaced in a dramatic way in the summer of 2010, when Shirley Sherrod, the black Georgia state director of rural development for the United States Department of Agriculture, was forced to resign under orders from the Obama White House.

During a speech that Sherrod had delivered at a meeting of the NAACP, she related her experience with a white farmer who came to her for help. Andrew Breitbart, the late conservative blogger, got hold of the tape of Sherrod's speech and, through selective editing, made it sound as though Sherrod had refused to help the farmer because he was white. In Breitbart's telling, Sherrod was a black racist. However, when the complete tape of Sherrod's speech was released, it became clear that she was nothing of the sort. In fact, she had worked hard to save the white farmer's land.

By firing Sherrod without looking into the matter more carefully, Obama once again revealed himself to be politically inept. Unknowingly, he had picked a fight with the wrong black person, for not only was Shirley Sherrod falsely maligned by the White House, but it turned out that her husband, Charles Sherrod, had played a significant role in the 1960s civil rights movement. Charles Sherrod had been a Freedom Rider along with John Lewis, a prominent member of the Student Nonviolent Coordinating Committee and a longtime Georgia congressman.

As might be expected, the African-American political elite quickly came to the defense of the Sherrods. "I've known these two individuals—the husband for more than fifty years and the wife for at least thirty-five, forty—and there's not a racist hair on their heads or anyplace else on their bodies," Congressman Lewis said.

"I don't think a single black person was consulted before Shirley Sherrod was fired—I mean, c'mon," said Congressman James Clyburn of South Carolina, who had ditched Hillary Clinton to support Obama in the 2008 Democratic primary campaign. "The president is getting hurt real bad. He needs some black people around him. . . . Some people over there [in the White House] are not sensitive at all about race. They really feel that the extent to which he allows himself to talk about race would tend to pigeonhole him or cost him support, when a lot of people saw his election as a way to get the issue behind us. I don't think people elected him to disengage on race. Just the opposite."

Eleanor Holmes Norton, the representative from the District of Columbia, concurred: "The president needs some advisers or friends who have a greater sense of the pulse of the African-American community, or who at least have been around the mulberry bush."

Never one to graciously admit his mistakes, Obama finally phoned Shirley Sherrod and spoke to her for a grudging seven minutes. Obama said he felt that the incident had been blown way out of proportion, and he refused to apologize personally for the national humiliation Sherrod had suffered. When he offered Sherrod another job in the Agriculture Department, she politely declined.

In the wake of the Sherrod incident, Maureen Dowd, usually a liberal voice on the op-ed page of the *New York Times*, unleashed a blistering rebuke of Obama.

"The Obama White House is too white," wrote Dowd.

> It has Barack Obama, raised in the Hawaiian hood and Indonesia, and Valerie Jarrett, who spent her early years in Iran. But unlike Bill Clinton, who never needed help fathoming Southern black culture, Obama lacks advisers who are descended from the central African-American experience, ones who understand "the slave thing," as a top black Democrat dryly puts it.... The president shouldn't give Sherrod her old job back. He

should give her a new job: Director of Black Outreach. This White House needs one.

━━━━━━━

The Sherrod Case was a turning point in relations between Obama and the black leadership. No longer were blacks willing to bite their tongues when speaking about the black president. By the summer of 2011, the Congressional Black Caucus was openly warning Obama that black voters were frustrated by his administration's unwillingness to address black joblessness, which was more than double the national average, and which rose as high as 40 percent in urban centers like Chicago and Detroit. The message was clear: although Obama would probably still get more than 90 percent of the African-American vote in 2012, he couldn't count on the kind of black turnout he had generated in 2008 to offset the white vote in swing states.

"I'm frustrated with the president, I'm frustrated with the Senate, I'm frustrated with the House," Representative Emanuel Cleaver II, a Missouri Democrat and chairman of the Congressional Black Caucus, said in an interview with the *Wall Street Journal*. "The president and his White House team [are] trying to minimize the discussion of race as it relates to job creation."

Emanuel Cleaver's complaint was echoed by Maxine Waters, a former chairman of the caucus. "The worry should be that are [black] people going to be enthusiastic about getting to the polls, or are they not going to be as enthusiastic."

Obama compounded his problem with African-Americans in August 2011, when he set off on a three-day bus tour through the Midwest to talk about his push to create jobs. With his approval ratings at an all-time low of 39 percent, Obama campaigned before all-white audiences in Minnesota, Iowa, and Illinois. This set off a chorus of criticism from black leaders, who wanted to know why the president had avoided African-American communities.

Stung by all this criticism, Obama appeared before the Congressional Black Caucus in September 2011 and gave a no-holds-barred speech chastising his critics. He told the attendees at the gathering to "take off your bedroom slippers, put on your marching shoes" and "stop complaining, stop grumbling, stop crying."

In response, Maxine Waters deftly put the president in his place. "I've never owned a pair of bedroom slippers," she said.

If relations between Obama and black politicians were touchy, they were downright contentious with black businessmen. I spoke with Harry C. Alford, the president and CEO of the National Black Chamber of Commerce, which represents the nearly two million black businesses in the United States.

"When Obama became president, we were all happy about the symbolism—America's first black president," Alford told me. "We didn't really care about his position or views on anything. We just wanted a black president no matter what. We should have been more careful, as his views on small business, especially black business, are counter to ours.

"His view of business is that it should be a few major corporations which are totally unionized and working with the government, which should also be massive and reaching every level of American society," Alford continued. "Thus, his first Executive Order was the reinstatement of Project Labor Agreements in government contracting. PLAs give labor unions an exclusive [option] in construction jobs—all participating firms must use union labor or, at least, pay union wages and abide by union rules. This activity, in effect, discriminates against blacks, Hispanics, and women per se, as trade unions deliberately under-employ them....

"President George W. Bush eliminated PLAs from federal contracting and his main reason was 'unions discriminate against small business, women, and minorities.' So here we were with the first black president who deliberately discriminates against small business, women, and minorities. How ironic!"

———

As he headed into his fourth year in office and began to gear up for his reelection campaign, Obama was forced to face an uncomfortable fact: he was profoundly unpopular with black leaders, who found him cold and distant, an inauthentic "brother." If he hoped to generate a large black voter turnout in 2012, something had to be done to counter this growing disenchantment. He had to rally his base.

Suddenly, I started hearing from prominent blacks, whose phone calls and emails to the White House had gone unanswered for three years.

"I wanted you to know that I finally got an invitation to the White House—I was asked to attend the White House Christmas party," one of Obama's severest black critics told me. Others confirmed that the White House had undertaken a full-court press to win black approval.

In January 2012, the president turned up at Harlem's Apollo Theater, the mecca of African-American culture, where he broke into the opening of Al Green's recording of "Let's Stay Together." A month later, he hosted a tribute to the blues at the White House and joined bluesmen B. B. King and Buddy Guy for the first few lines of "Sweet Home Chicago."

"It makes the president more likable because it's humanizing," said Mark McKinnon, a Republican political strategist and a onetime Nashville songwriter. "Just the fact that he tried to sing in public was a single. That he sang well was a double. That he didn't sing 'America the Beautiful' was a triple. That he sang Al Green was a home run.… Not saying that he could win *American Idol*, but he's got some decent pipes. History will judge his presidency, but it's probably not a stretch to say he may be the best crooner to occupy the Oval Office."

PART IV

THE OBAMA DOCTRINE

---

*The United States under Barack Obama
is less assertive, less dominant, less power-minded,
less focused on the American people's particular
interests, and less concerned about preserving
U.S. freedom of action.*

—Douglas J. Feith and Seth Cropsey, "The Obama Doctrine
Defined," *Commentary* magazine, July 2011

CHAPTER 17

THE WAR ON GENERAL JONES

They're a bunch of Chicago thugs.

—Diane Jones, wife of General James Jones,
speaking about Barack Obama's inner circle

D iane Jones had reason to be bitter.

No one in the Obama White House had a more distinguished record of service to his country than her husband, James Logan Jones Jr. The six-foot-four, plainspoken, retired four-star Marine Corps general was a decorated combat veteran of the Vietnam War, a former commandant of the Marine Corps, the first Marine Corps general to serve as supreme allied commander in Europe, and a trusted military adviser to both Democratic and Republican presidents. And yet, within months of being appointed as Obama's first national security adviser, Jones became the victim of a snarky whispering campaign by White House aides, who spread word in the media that he was so detached from his job that he bicycled home to McLean, Virginia, for lunch and left work early.

As a rule, Jones followed John Wayne's advice in *She Wore a Yellow Ribbon*: "Never apologize, never explain—it's a sign of weakness." But things became so nasty in the West Wing that, less than four months into his tenure, he took the unusual step of defending himself in the press: "I'm here by 7 o'clock in the morning and I go home at 7, 7:30 at night; that's a fairly reasonable day if you're properly organized.... There is a generational thing here," continued Jones, who at age sixty-five was some twenty years older than most of his staff. "There is a process thing here. I'm used to staffs, and I'm used to certain order. I'm used to people having certain roles. And so there's a very natural adjustment period.... When I first went into the Oval Office, I didn't expect six other people from the [National Security Council] to go with me."

Asked by a *New York Times* reporter about the behavior of young Obama officials who prided themselves on staying at the White House until late at night, Jones snapped: "Congratulations. To me that means you're not organized."

The late Richard Holbrooke, the most talented diplomat of his generation and Obama's representative to Afghanistan and Pakistan, respected Jones. In response to charges that Jones delegated too much responsibility to his subordinates, Holbrooke pointed out that, as a Marine, Jones "believes in team-building" and had produced "a sophisticated, multilayer decision structure at the National Security Council that did not exist before." Holbrooke didn't suffer fools or amateurs gladly, and as far as he was concerned, hiring someone as mature and experienced as Jim Jones and then not using him properly displayed a lack of executive sense on the part of Obama. But Holbrooke's defense of Jones fell on deaf ears. Holbrooke had been a Hillary Clinton loyalist during the primary campaign and, like Jones, he was treated as an outsider by the inbred claque of Obamans.

Jones's brutal turf fights with Obama's inner circle were chronicled in Bob Woodward's book, *Obama's Wars*, for which Jones was a major source. The general complained to Woodward that the political team Obama had imported from Chicago— Rahm Emanuel, David Axelrod, Valerie Jarrett, and Robert Gibbs—made it virtually impossible for him to do his job. The Chicagoans even went so far as to block his access to the president. He described them to Woodward as "water bugs," the "Politburo," and "the Mafia."

A clash of personalities was only part of Jones's problems. For all of Obama's talk about being open-minded and willing to listen to competing ideas, he was only comfortable with people who shared his view of America as a less predominant power in a multipolar world. Though a registered Democrat, Jones was non-ideological; he was neither a hawk nor a prophet of American doom. He was a warrior-diplomat in the tradition of Generals George C. Marshall and Maxwell Taylor, and the sorry saga of his tenure in the White House said volumes about how Barack Obama conducted America's foreign policy.

Jones hardly knew Obama when he was appointed to head the National Security Council. In fact, the two men had met only twice. The first time was in 2005, when then Senator Obama's foreign policy aide, Mark Lippert, arranged a meeting between the two men. Obama and Jones met again in the fall of 2008, when President-elect Obama asked Jones to become his chief national security adviser. Despite his low-key manner and the deference he showed to the young, inexperienced president, Jones was never able to bond with Obama the way his predecessors in the NSC job, Condoleezza Rice and Stephen Hadley, had bonded with George W. Bush.

There were signs from the beginning that Jones's calm, systematic approach to problems did not fit the frenetic, highly politicized atmosphere in the Obama White House. That lesson was brought home to Jones when he was asked to phone Marine General Anthony Zinni, a former commander of Central Command and a friend of thirty years, and offer him a key job in the new administration.

"Jones... asked if I would be willing to serve as ambassador to Iraq or in one of the envoy jobs, on the Middle East peace process," Zinni recalled. "I said yes. Then [right after the inauguration], Jones called and said, 'We talked to the secretary of state, and everybody would like to offer you the Iraq job.' I said yes. The [vice] president called and congratulated me."

The next thing Zinni knew he was asked to meet with Secretary of State Hillary Clinton in her office at the State Department.

When he showed up, Clinton introduced him to Deputy Secretary of State James Steinberg and Undersecretary of State for Political Affairs William Burns. "She asked me my views on Iraq," Zinni said. "She said to Burns and Steinberg, 'We've got to move quickly. [Ambassador Ryan] Crocker is leaving [Iraq]. We've got to get someone in there and get the paperwork done and hearings.... Lots to do to get ready to go.'"

Zinni expected to get a call the next day, and when he didn't, he phoned Undersecretary Bill Burns.

"To make a long story short, I kept getting blown off all week," Zinni said. "Meantime, I was rushing to put my personal things in order.... I was beginning to set up to resign from boards and put my financial house in order, kiss my wife goodbye. And nothing happened.... Finally, nobody was telling me anything. I called Jones... several times. I finally got through late in the evening. I asked Jones, 'What's going on?' And Jones said, 'We decided on Chris Hill.' I said, 'No one told me. If I hadn't called you, I'd have read about it in the *Washington Post*.' And Jones said, 'I didn't know.'"

Jones was mortified by the way the Obama White House had treated his old friend and fellow Marine. As things turned out, it was only the first of many humiliations he suffered while working with Barack Obama.

Despite his considerable prestige, Jones was not permitted to pick his own staff. What's more, he was rarely allowed to see the president alone. When he went to the Oval Office, he was usually accompanied by a phalanx of aides, including three political operatives who had played key roles in Obama's 2008 presidential campaign: Jones's chief of staff, Mark Lippert; his deputy, Tom Donilon, who had coached Obama for his debates against John McCain; and Denis McDonough, the director of strategic communications. At times, this group was expanded to include Hillary Clinton, Valerie Jarrett, David Axelrod, Rahm Emanuel, and, on rare occasions, Michelle Obama. Most of the attendees were not foreign policy experts. However, that didn't stop people like Valerie Jarrett from expressing opinions on matters about which they knew little or nothing.

Making Jones part of a large and diffuse group signaled to everyone in Washington that he didn't have Obama's ear on foreign policy. His influence was further diminished by the way Obama conducted meetings on foreign policy. He liked to do most of the talking. Others in the room, including Jones, were there to listen and agree, even on military matters like the deployment of aircraft carrier groups.

Leslie Gelb, the former president of the Council on Foreign Relations, told me that no president had taken more personal control over foreign policy than Obama. "This is an Obama-centric decision-making operation. In other administrations, a lot of decisions were made below the presidential level. But Obama shapes most policies. He takes pen to paper and writes decision papers. Usually presidents have other things to do than sit down and write a document that takes an inordinate amount of time. But Obama makes the calls on most every subject and with a degree of personal intensity."

Both in the Oval Office and at National Security Council meetings in the Situation Room, Obama seemed to pass quickly over Jones in favor of his deputy, Tom Donilon. Understandably enough, this annoyed Jones. He had little use for Donilon, a Democratic Party insider who had worked as an aide for Jimmy Carter and Walter Mondale, and was a former Washington lobbyist and executive at Fannie Mae.

Jones was particularly annoyed by Donilon's habit of making derogatory remarks about American military commanders in Iraq and Afghanistan—two theaters of war that Donilon had never bothered to visit. On one occasion, Jones told Donilon that, given his lack of overseas experience, "You have no credibility with the military." But Donilon was protected by Rahm Emanuel (who openly snubbed Jones in favor of Donilon) and by Vice President Joe Biden (Donilon's wife, Cathy, was chief of staff to Biden's wife, Jill).

Not everyone in the administration was sold on Donilon. No less a player than Secretary of Defense Robert Gates agreed with Jones that Donilon had a poor record of working with the military. But that didn't stop Obama from appointing Donilon, who was a favorite with the Democratic Party's leftwing base, to succeed as national security adviser when Jones finally decided to pack it in after nineteen vicious months.

CHAPTER 18

MIND-MELD

I'm a genocide chick.

—Samantha Power, senior director for multilateral affairs,
National Security Council

The shameful treatment of General Jones pointed to a neglected fact about Barack Obama's foreign policy— namely, that it was as ideologically skewed to the Left as his domestic policy. This shouldn't have come as a surprise to anyone who had followed Obama's ascent to power on the left flank of the Democratic Party. Obama won his party's nomination at least in part because he promised to end the Bush-era wars, and put a stop to "torture" and the imprisonment of terrorists without trial. Equally important, he pledged to re-establish American foreign policy on a whole new set of lofty-sounding but dubious liberal principles.

Obama's approach was a rupture with the past. For several decades during the Cold War, there had been general agreement among Democrats and Republicans about the underpinnings of American national security. As Douglas Feith and Seth Cropsey wrote in an important article in *Commentary* magazine, most Americans, both left and right, subscribed to the following ideas:

> American interests, rather than global interests, should predominate in U.S. policymaking. American leadership, as traditionally defined, is indispensible to promoting the interests of the United States and our key partners, who are our fellow democracies. American power is generally a force for good in the world. And, as important as international cooperation can be, the U.S. president should cherish American sovereignty and defend his ability to act independently to protect the American people and their interests.

Obama challenged all of these basic assumptions. In his view, American power had done more harm than good. Global interests should generally come before American interests. International law should be taken into consideration by American courts. Washington should hesitate to act without the cooperation of the world community. America had an obligation to extend an olive branch to everyone, including its sworn enemies in North Korea and Iran.

The Obama Doctrine, as it came to be known, was given official status in the administration's National Security Strategy

(NSS), a 30,000-word document, required by an act of Congress, which repudiated President George W. Bush's "unilateralism" and argued in favor of "counting more on U.S. allies."

"Most notably," wrote Miles E. Taylor in *World Politics Review*, "Obama's NSS downplays the promotion of American values when compared to those of his predecessors. The words 'freedom' and 'liberty,' for example appear only 14 times in the text. This is stunning when compared to the Bush NSS, released in 2006, which stressed those core principles no less than 110 times—and in a document that was substantially shorter than Obama's.... The Obama NSS declares that 'American values' like freedom and democratic governance are 'the essential sources of our strength.' Why, then, are they given comparably short shrift in the document itself?

"The answer," Taylor continued, "is that the Obama team has been consistently cool toward the idea of democracy promotion since winning the White House, partly to avoid the appearance of being similar to Bush and partly to avoid ruffling the feathers of rogue regimes with which it hoped to engage."

All of this struck a chord with members of Obama's leftwing base, who had wailed and gnashed their teeth over George W. Bush's policies of preemptive wars and nation building. However, having bought Obama's do-gooder rhetoric, liberals were thrown into a state of shock when he increased the number of American troops in Afghanistan, failed to end the war in Iraq immediately (he merely modified the Bush administration's timeline for withdrawal), and upped the ante on Bush's unmanned drone war against terrorists. What's more, liberals were rendered practically speechless by the fact that, under Obama, America's relationship with Europe turned out to be no better than it had been under Bush, and that—despite all his ballyhooed diplomatic overtures to the Islamic world—polling showed that Islamic countries actually felt more hostile toward the United States than before.

Naturally enough, conservatives did not suffer the same disillusionment and buyer's remorse. Many of them had forecast disaster for Obama, and they were not surprised when their predictions came true. To conservatives who championed a muscular foreign policy of *Realpolitik*, the Obama Doctrine was a confused hodgepodge at best and *The Complete Idiot's Guide to Foreign Policy* at worst.

The Obama Doctrine wasn't born full-blown from the head of the newly elected president. The ideas that animated his worldview could be traced back to the end of the Cold War and a debate that broke out in the ranks of the Democratic Party over the proper role of America in the world.

By the early 1990s, liberal Democrats were raising questions about the limits of American power and the willingness of the American people to act as the policemen of the world. Alan Tonelson, a research director for the liberal Economic Strategy Institute, argued in the quarterly *Foreign Affairs* that "the superpower role that America has played since 1945 is now not only too expensive and risky for the public taste, but it is also unnecessary." And in May 1993, just four months into Bill Clinton's first term, Peter Tarnoff, the undersecretary of state and the third-ranking official in the Clinton State Department, went a good deal further than that.

In a lunch with the Overseas Writers Club, a group of diplomatic reporters, Tarnoff said: "Our economic interests are paramount," and given America's limited resources, the United States must "define the extent of its commitment commensurate with those realities—this may on occasion fall short of what some Americans would like and others would hope for."

Dubbed the Tarnoff Doctrine by the media, this policy suggested that the Clinton administration expected to withdraw America from many of its customary foreign leadership roles. Although that was not exactly what Tarnoff had in mind—he pointed out that the United States would continue to defend its national interests alone when *directly* challenged—his interview made a splash in several major newspapers. For instance, the *Los Angeles Times* reported: "President Clinton's decision to defer to European views on Bosnia-Herzegovina reflects a deliberate shift in a new, post-Cold War model of American power: limited by economic problems, modest in style and rarely exercised unilaterally, a senior State Department official said Tuesday."

Such stories created an instant outcry from moderates and conservatives. The State Department's public relations flack, Tom Donilon—the same Tom Donilon who would later replace Jim Jones as Obama's national security adviser—tried to talk the *Washington Post* out of running a story on Tarnoff's comments. When that didn't work, Secretary of State Warren Christopher rushed to disavow Tarnoff's statements and assuage the fears expressed by America's allies around the world. But the damage had already been done; world leaders expected the United States to behave in a weaker fashion.

As things turned out, the ideas behind the Tarnoff Doctrine were commonplace among liberals in America's leading universities and think tanks. "Their community is Barack Obama's community," Feith and Cropsey wrote in *Commentary*. "These are the people with whom he studied and with whom he worked as a faculty colleague. He drew heavily on his fellow progressive academics to fill top jobs in his administration, and it is evident they have helped shape his understanding of American history, his perception of international affairs, and his strategy for transforming America's purpose and role in the world."

When it came to foreign affairs, no one had a more profound influence on Barack Obama's thinking than Samantha Power, who burst upon the foreign policy scene in 2003 with the publication of her book, *A Problem from Hell*, which indicted America and other democracies for being "bystanders to genocide." A glamorous Harvard professor with a mane of lustrous red hair, Power hobnobbed with Hollywood stars and other liberal celebrities, and once posed in a teal gown and high heels for *Men's Vogue*, which described her as a "Harvard brainiac who can boast both a Pulitzer Prize and a mean jump shot (ask George Clooney)."

As an academic, Power had steered clear of politicians—that is, until she met Barack Obama in 2005, became smitten with him, and volunteered to work in his Senate office. It was an instant mind-meld, and Power became one of Obama's closest foreign policy advisers. They enjoyed a special relationship and frequently texted via their BlackBerries. Power authored a memo titled "Conventional Washington versus the Change We Need," in which she buttressed the foundations of the Obama Doctrine. "Barack Obama's judgment is right," she wrote. "The conventional wisdom is wrong. We need a new era of tough, principled and engaged American diplomacy to deal with 21st century challenges."

In the midst of the 2008 Democratic primary campaign, Power embarked on an international tour to promote her book, *Chasing the Flame*. She told a reporter from *The Scotsman*: "We fucked up in Ohio... and Hillary is going to town on it, because she knows Ohio's the only place they can win.... She is a monster, too—that's off the record—she is stooping to anything.... If you are poor and she is telling you some story about how Obama is going to take your job away, maybe it will be more effective. The amount of deceit she has put forward is really unattractive."

Though Power quickly apologized for calling Hillary a monster, she was forced to cancel her book tour and resign from the Obama campaign. The neoconservative *Weekly Standard* noted: "It might have been the most ill-starred book tour since the invention of movable type." But it was impossible to keep Power down, and when Obama won the White House, he made her a member of his transition team, then appointed her to the National Security Council, where she serves as special assistant to the president and runs the Office of Multilateral Affairs and Human Rights.

"U.S. foreign policy has to be rethought," Power argued. "It needs not tweaking but overhauling.... Instituting a doctrine of mea culpa would enhance our credibility by showing that American decision-makers do not endorse the sins of their predecessors. When [then German Chancellor Willy] Brandt went down on one knee in the Warsaw ghetto, his gesture was gratifying to World War II survivors, but it was also ennobling and cathartic for Germany. Would such an approach be futile for the United States?"

Power's answer to her own question was clear: she wanted Obama to get "down on one knee" and seek pardon for the sins of American foreign policy. But that alone, Power warned, would not be enough to undo the harm America had inflicted on the world, especially in the Middle East. In order to solve the problems of the Middle East, Obama had to disentangle the United States from Israel and not worry about the so-called Jewish Lobby.

"So much of [the debate over the Middle East] is about: 'Is [Obama] going to be good for the Jews,'" she complained, apparently unaware that such a remark could be interpreted as anti-Semitic. Obama, she went on to say, had to be willing to "alienate a domestic [Jewish] constituency of tremendous political and financial import: it may more crucially mean sacrificing... billions of dollars, not in servicing Israel's military, but actually investing

in the state of Palestine.... America's important historic relationship with Israel has often led foreign policy decision-makers to
defer reflexively to Israeli security assessments, and to replicate
Israeli tactics, which, as the war in Lebanon... demonstrated,
can turn out to be counter-productive."

Samantha Power's history of America's Middle East policy
was a complete distortion, but her radical leftwing attitudes were
reflected in Obama's antagonism toward Israel.

In April 2009, when Barack Obama attended the G20 Summit in London and greeted the King of Saudi Arabia with a full
bow from the waist, it was plain for all to see that Samantha's
Power's ideas had prevailed over *Miss Manners*' book of eti-
quette, which strongly advised Americans "not to bow or curtsy
to a foreign monarch." And when Obama went to Cairo two
months later and addressed the Muslim world in a landmark
speech, foreign-policy cognoscenti could detect the echoes of
Samantha Power in the president's words.

"I've come here to seek a new beginning between the United
States and Muslims around the world," Obama declared in
Cairo. The poor relations between Americans and Muslims had
little to do with the shockingly bad behavior of dictatorial Arab
regimes and their obstinate refusal to recognize the right of Israel
to exist, he said. Rather, the strains were the fault of Western
"colonialism that denied rights and opportunities to many Muslims." (He made no mention of the fact that the Ottoman Empire

ruled the Arab world for 600 years—far longer and with a more detrimental effect than the West.)

Obama presented himself as a paragon of religious tolerance in contrast to the narrow-minded people "in my country [who] view Islam as inevitably hostile... to human rights." (He made no mention of how existing policies in the Arab world discriminated against women.) The response by President George W. Bush to the September 11, 2001, attacks on America, he lamented, "led us to act contrary to our ideals." No longer would America seek to impose its will on others, because "any world order that elevates one nation or group of people over another will inevitably fail."

"Barack Obama's mention of 'nearly seven million American Muslims' in the course of his rambling and complex 6,000-word address to the Muslim world from Cairo symbolizes the whole message," blogged Daniel Pipes, the respected editor of *Middle East Quarterly*. "Study after study has found that demographic figure about three times too high. But Islamist organizations like the Council on American-Islamic Relations and the Islamic Society of North America relentlessly promote the notion of seven or even ten million American Muslims. Obama's acceptance of their version amounts to a giveaway, a cheap way to win the approbation of Islamists who so widely influence Muslim opinion.

"'Giveaway,' indeed, defines the whole speech—inexpensive nods, tips of the hat, and salutations to win Muslim favor without initiating new approaches or embarking on new policies," Pipes continued. "The speech confirms Obama's personal efforts... as well as the established practice of American political leaders to promote Islam, tell Muslims what their religion really means, avoid references to radical Islam, and excoriate violent Islamism while accepting the non-violent variety."

Obama was so anxious to curry favor with the Muslim community that his Justice Department prohibited the mention of "Islam" or "Islamic terror" in federal law enforcement training manuals. In addition, Obama instructed his advisers to remove the term "Islamic extremism" from the central document outlining America's National Security Strategy. The change in approach was dramatized when Paul Stockton, the Assistant Secretary of Defense for Homeland Defense and Security Affairs, appeared before a joint Senate/House Homeland Security hearing. He was asked by Representative Dan Lungren, a former attorney general of California, about the source of the threat to America and its troops. The exchange went as follows:

Representative Daniel Lungren (R-CA): Secretary Stockton, are we at war with violent Islamist extremism?

Mr. Stockton: No, sir. We are at war with al Qaeda, its affiliates.

Rep. Lungren: Okay, I understand that. My question is, is violent Islamist extremism at war with us?

Mr. Stockton: No, sir. We are being attacked by al Qaeda and its allies.

Rep. Lungren: Is al Qaeda—can it be described as being an exponent of violent Islamist extremism?

Mr. Stockton: They—al Qaeda are murderers with an ideological agenda.

Rep. Lungren: No, I—that's not my question. That wasn't my question. My question was, is al Qaeda acting out violent Islamist extremism?

Mr. Stockton: Al Qaeda is a violent organization dedicated to overthrowing the values that we intend to advance.

Rep. Lungren: So is it yes or no?

Mr. Stockton: Can I hear the question again? I'll make it as clear as I can. We are not at war with Islam. And it is not—

Rep. Lungren: I didn't ask that—I did not ask that, sir. I asked whether we're at war with violent Islamist extremism. That's my question.

Mr. Stockton: No, we're at war with al Qaeda and its affiliates.

CHAPTER 19

THE RISE OF THE HUMANITARIAN VULCANS

Leading from behind.... That's not a slogan designed for signs at the 2012 Democratic Convention, but it does accurately describe the balance that Obama now seems to be finding. It's a different definition of leadership than America is known for, and it comes from two unspoken beliefs: that the relative power of the U.S. is declining, as rivals like China rise, and that the U.S. is reviled in many parts of the world.

—Ryan Lizza, *The New Yorker*

The crisis over Libya, which began in February 2011 and lasted for seven long months, accentuated the glaring inconsistencies in the Obama Doctrine. Vice President Biden, Secretary of Defense Robert Gates, and National Security Adviser Tom Donilon all urged Obama *not* to intervene in the Libyan civil war.

By ignoring their counsel, the president violated three of the main principles supporting the Obama Doctrine:

- **Principle No. 1.** America will lead the world in supporting democracy and fostering international human rights.

  Violation of Principle No. 1. As the *Wall Street Journal* pointed out: "No one can any longer doubt the U.S. determination not to act before the Italians do, or until the Saudis approve, or without a U.N. resolution. This White House is forthright for followership."

- **Principle No. 2.** America will not get involved in foreign military adventures unless its national interest is directly challenged.

  Violation of Principle No. 2. In Libya, Obama plunged the United States into a long and costly military campaign that had little strategic value and less public support.

- **Principle No. 3.** America will not repeat George W. Bush's mistake of invading an Islamic country like Iraq in order to topple a brutal dictatorship.

  Violation of Principle No. 3. The military campaign in Libya was aimed at deposing the dictatorship of Muammar Gaddafi. In that respect, it was Bush Redux.

Given the violations of his own principles, why did Obama go into Libya?

"There has been much speculation that the intervention in Libya was about oil," wrote George Friedman, the founder and CEO of the global intelligence newsletter *Stratfor*. "All such interventions, such as those in Kosovo and Haiti, are examined for hidden purposes. Perhaps it was about oil in this case, but Gaddafi was happily shipping oil to Europe, so intervening to ensure that it continues makes no sense."

In fact, the whole exercise in Libya made no sense unless it was viewed through the prism of domestic politics. Opinion polls at the beginning of 2011 showed that Obama's confused and feeble response to the Arab Spring had seriously undermined his credibility. His dithering amateurism added to the growing impression that he lacked the courage of his convictions, and was unable to provide decisive and resolute leadership. An anonymous Hillary Clinton aide told *The Daily* that the secretary of state, who until then had meticulously avoided criticizing Obama, was fed up with "a president who can't make up his mind." Hillary reportedly referred to Obama as "a president who can't decide if today is Tuesday or Wednesday." She also likened Obama and his advisers to "a bunch of amateurs" in their handling of Gaddafi.

"Since the beginning of the Arab Spring, the Obama administration had been grappling with how the United States should respond to the wave of democratic uprisings sweeping the region, first in Tunisia, then in Egypt, Yemen, Bahrain, Libya, Morocco, and Syria," wrote Michael Hastings in *Rolling Stone* magazine.

…[O]nce those governments actually began to fall, the Obama administration was slow to distance itself from the oil-rich autocrats the U.S. had supported for decades. In Egypt, Vice President Joe Biden downplayed the democratic revolt, saying that he didn't consider Hosni Mubarak a "dictator." In Bahrain—home of the U.S. 5th Fleet—the administration looked the other way as the royal family allowed the military to violently crush peaceful street protests. In Yemen, the U.S. chose not to intervene when the country's military fired into crowds calling for the president's resignation. To Arab protesters, Obama's "new beginning" [proclaimed in his Cairo speech] seemed more like the same old American realpolitik that had long dominated the Middle East.

From all appearances, Obama was fiddling while the Arab world burned. But behind the scenes, a fierce battle for influence over policy was brewing at the White House. Among Obama's foreign policy advisers, Samantha Power, the far-out leftist firebrand, complained that the administration's cautious, first-do-no-harm approach to the Arab Spring had effectively sidelined her in White House councils. She said she'd been relegated to "doing rinky-dink do-gooder stuff," such as advocating on behalf of beleaguered Christians in Iraq, and no longer had as much access to the president. She was itching to get back into the fray, and she saw an opportunity in Libya.

Power argued that Obama had ample justification to intervene in Libya under the humanitarian doctrine of "R2P"—shorthand for "Responsibility to Protect." She outlined the basic tenets of R2P in a speech she delivered at the International Symposium on Preventing Genocide and Mass Atrocities in Paris.

"What, concretely, should we—we governments, we advocates, we historians, we educators, we museum curators, we citizens, we NGOs—what should we be doing—and what should we be doing differently—in order to further reduce the likelihood of crimes that shock the conscience?" she said. "In his National Security Strategy... President Obama made clear that our effort to responsibly end the war in Iraq and defeat al-Qaeda in Afghanistan must be matched with a vigorous commitment to prevent mass atrocities. His National Security Strategy included the most detailed summation of the U.S. government's approach to mass atrocity that an American president has given to date.... "

In the words of *Stratfor*'s George Friedman, Samantha Power was advocating what amounted to a policy of Immaculate Intervention. "I call humanitarian wars immaculate intervention," said Friedman, "because most advocates want to see the outcome limited to preventing war crimes, not extended to include regime change or the imposition of alien values. They want a war of immaculate intentions surgically limited to a singular end without other consequences. And this is where the doctrine of humanitarian war unravels.

"Regardless of intention, any intervention favors the weaker side," he continued.

> If the side were not weak, it would not be facing mass murder: it could protect itself. Given that the intervention

must be military, there must be an enemy.... My unease
with humanitarian intervention is not that I don't think
the intent is good and the end moral. It is that the intent
frequently gets lost and the moral end is not achieved....
A doctrine of humanitarian warfare that demands an
immaculate intervention will fail because the desire to do
good is an insufficient basis for war.... In the end, the
ultimate dishonesties of humanitarian war are the claims
that "this won't hurt much" and "it will be over fast."

Neither Samantha Power nor her ideological bedfellow, Susan
Rice, the U.S. ambassador to the United Nations, was swayed by
the arguments against humanitarian intervention. On the contrary, Rice confessed that she felt guilty for having failed to push
for intervention in Rwanda when she served on the National
Security Council under Bill Clinton.

"[Rice and Power's] formative experience in foreign policy
wasn't Iraq or Afghanistan, but memories of the ethnic cleansing
in the Balkans and Rwanda during the 1990s, a period in which
they firmly believed that the United States had failed in its responsibilities to other countries," *Rolling Stone*'s Michael Hastings
noted. "They would now be to Obama what the neoconservatives
had been to Bush: ardent advocates for war in the name of a
grander cause. Libya, in effect, represent[ed] the rise of the
humanitarian Vulcans."

But Rice and Power wouldn't have gotten very far if they
hadn't been joined by a third woman, Secretary of State Hillary
Clinton. By the second week of March, with Gaddafi's forces on

the outskirts of Benghazi, the second largest city in Libya, and the rebels on the brink of collapse, France, England, and the members of the Arab League were clamoring for action. Convinced that there was a coalition of the willing, Hillary Clinton threw her support behind the hawkish Rice and Power, and urged Obama to begin a bombing campaign.

Obama hesitated. He was under pressure from opposing wings in the Democratic Party. "Humanitarian idealists" urged him not to stand idly by and watch a repeat in Libya of the 1994 Rwanda massacre, which had been a blotch on the record of Bill Clinton. "Realists" argued just as convincingly that, in the wake of Iraq and Afghanistan, the United States couldn't afford to plunge into a third war in the Islamic world; such an action would reap a whirlwind of Arab hatred.

What was he to do?

In typical Obama fashion, he devised a policy that muddied the difference. He would favor war, without going to war. He would support a NATO air campaign against Gaddafi under the auspices of the United Nations, but he wouldn't commit significant American airpower to the battle even though the United States was the most important member of NATO. He would support a policy of regime change in Libya, but he wouldn't declare that as a goal of American policy. He would publicly maintain his continuing opposition to the Bush-era policy of nation building, but he would help create a new government in Libya. He would reject America's post-World War II role as the initiator and guarantor of world order and, in the now-infamous words of one of his advisers, "lead from behind."

In certain quarters, Obama's Libyan operation was counted a major achievement. Despite the alarming rise of revolutionary Islamism in Libya and other countries convulsed by the Arab Spring, I've heard people express the opinion that Obama has proved himself to be a better foreign policy president than a domestic policy president.

In view of Obama's pitiful record on the home front, that may not be saying much. Nonetheless, the notion that Obama has been more effective overseas than at home seems paradoxical when the Obama administration boasts of a policy of international retrenchment and believes that the era of American leadership is, and should be, long past. Under the Obama presidency, America has become weaker than at any time since the end of the Cold War. Our Navy has been cut in half and is growing smaller. Our Army and Marine Corps have 600,000 fewer troops, and will soon have even fewer. Our military budget is being slashed by billions. Our adversaries are gaining military, economic, diplomatic, and technological advantage over the United States thanks to a president who is viewed as weak.

And yet, there are those who argue that Obama has scored several major foreign policy successes. In fact, their view has become part of the conventional wisdom on the Left, especially in the mainstream media. With little to cheer about at home, the media have given Obama a standing ovation over his decision to green-light the daring raid by the Navy SEALs that killed Osama bin Laden, his stepped-up unmanned drone strikes and special-operations campaigns that have decimated al Qaeda's leadership, and his "immaculate intervention" in Libya, which ended with the death of Muammar Gaddafi.

What the media miss is that a series of ad hoc military operations do not add up to a successful foreign policy. Effective diplomacy requires something that is sorely missing in Barack Obama's foreign policy—a coherent philosophy and worldview. Put another way, Obama lacks faith in the goodness of American leadership.

"The present world order was largely shaped by American power and reflects American interests and preferences," writes Robert Kagan, a foreign policy commentator at the Brookings Institution and author of *The World America Made*. "If the balance shifts in the direction of other nations, the world order will change to suit their interests and preferences. Nor can we assume that all the great powers in a post-American world would agree on the benefits of preserving the present order, or have the capacity to preserve it, even if they wanted to....

"International order is not an evolution; it is an imposition," Kagan continues. "It is the domination of one vision over others—in America's case, the domination of free-market and democratic principles, together with an international system that supports them. The present system will last only as long as those who favor it retain the will and capacity to defend it."

In the argument over whether Barack Obama has been a better foreign policy president than a domestic policy president, his record is the clincher. Judged by the ambitious goals he set for himself when he became president, he cannot claim to have achieved a single lasting policy objective in any area of the world that is of vital interest to the United States.

Rather than provide the kind of American leadership that once created the Marshall Plan and the Truman Doctrine, he has watched as a helpless bystander as the European Union has disintegrated. After nearly ten years of war in Iraq, he has undertaken a strategic withdrawal from the Middle East, leaving a vacuum that is certain to be filled by our sworn enemies in Iran. He called Afghanistan "a war of necessity," dispatched an additional 30,000 troops there, but foolishly set a date certain to bring America's troops home, thus creating yet another vacuum in an explosive part of the world. He has done little or nothing to stem the rise of China as a military power in the Far East. His ambivalent policy toward the mullahs in Iran and their ambition to become a nuclear power could only be described as an uncertain trumpet.

The Obama Doctrine with its two corollaries—"leading from behind" and "Responsibility to Protect"—is naïve, simplistic, and superficial. If further proof of this were needed, it came in the early months of 2012, when Bashar al-Assad began slaughtering his civilian opponents in Syria, which unlike Libya is of vital strategic importance to the United States, because Syria's regime is allied to both Russia and Iran.

"If the responsibility to protect civilians is a legitimate part of international law, why would it apply to Libya and not to Syria?" Steven Erlanger asked in the *New York Times*. "Why shouldn't the world intervene in what is already a one-sided civil war? Without a robust intervention, what happens to the momentum and principles of the Arab Spring? Will Western calls for democracy and equal rights suffer and help radical Islamists rise to power?"

Several leading Republicans called on the Obama administration to act. But the voices of the "humanitarian Vulcans"—Samantha Power, Susan Rice, and Hillary Clinton—were effectively silenced when Russia and China vetoed a Security Council resolution aimed at aiding the Syrian rebels and toppling the Assad regime. Without the fig leaf of international cooperation, which would allow the timorous Obama administration to lead from behind, Obama remained frozen in inaction. His refusal to take the lead in Syria to save civilian lives made a sham of "Responsibility to Protect," the guiding moral principle behind the Obama Doctrine.

As in past crises, the one in Syria demonstrated that Obama and his foreign policy team were bound by a narrow, cramped worldview. They envision a world of declining American power and the emergence of a new world order that will contain a half dozen major powers—the United States, Europe, China, Japan, Russia, and India. However, such a highly competitive, dangerous multipolar world is not inevitable. It will only materialize if the United States lets it. Obama should be more careful what he wishes for.

PART V

A ONE-TERM PROPOSITION?

One nice thing about the situation I find myself in is that I will be held accountable. You know, I've got four years.... If I don't have this done in three years, then there's going to be a one-term proposition.

—Barack Obama

CHAPTER 20

THE "NEW OBAMA"

*[Obama] needs to take a Valium before he comes in
and talks to Republicans. He's pretty thin-skinned.*

—Republican Senator Pat Roberts of Kansas

There is an old saying that nothing prepares a person to be president. Nowadays, a lot of liberals resort to this cliché as a way of excusing Barack Obama for the serial failures of his nearly four years in office. After all, liberals argue, if no one ever arrives at the White House with the requisite skills and talents to carry out the duties of the modern presidency, how can Obama be faulted for a first term that has been characterized by false starts and failed experiments? At least he tried.

But presidents don't get points for trying. What's more, the hackneyed saying that *all* presidents are unsuited for office is simply not true. It certainly wasn't true of George Washington, Abraham Lincoln, Franklin Roosevelt, Dwight Eisenhower, and Ronald Reagan. All of *them* were eminently suited for the presidency, because they had the temperament, management skills, and vision to tackle the job.

What *is* invariably true about our presidents is that the most successful ones grow in office. During the Civil War, Lincoln went through five commanders in the East before he settled on Ulysses S. Grant. In an assessment of John Kennedy, his speechwriter Theodore Sorensen noted: "If one extraordinary quality stood out among the many, it was the quality of continued growth. In November 1963, he had learned more about the uses and limitation of power, about the men on whom he could depend, about the adversaries and evils he faced, and about the tools and techniques of policy." The historian Arthur Schlesinger Jr. seconded the motion. "Kennedy," he said, "made his share of mistakes. But Kennedy never lost the capacity to learn from his mistakes. Each year he became a better president."

Can the same be said of Barack Obama?

Has he learned from his mistakes?

Has he become a better president?

The answer to these questions will strike many readers of this book as all too clear. I can just hear them chanting in unison: "No! *No!* NO!"

Nonetheless, the subject cannot be so easily dismissed. It is one thing for conservatives to view Obama as an irremediable political delinquent and bungling amateur who is hopelessly out of his depth. It is quite another thing to say of Obama, as Talleyrand was supposed to have said of the Bourbons, that he has "learned nothing and forgotten nothing." Indeed, the outcome of the 2012 presidential election may well be decided in Obama's favor if independent swing voters can be convinced that he has grown in office and deserves a second chance.

To shed light on the subject of Obama's "growth," I interviewed dozens of people in government, media, academia, and business. More than a few of them had worked in the Obama White House or in previous administrations. Others had studied Obama and his predecessors as reporters, writers, and historians.

My first round of interviews was with members of the White House press corps. It will come as no surprise to readers that there aren't many avowed conservatives in this group. Nor will readers be shocked to learn that most of the men and women who cover Obama on a day-to-day basis are, to put it charitably, partial toward Obama and are inclined to believe that he has demonstrated a real ability to grow and adapt.

This may be a classic case of the wish being father to the thought. But there is no denying the fact that most members of the White House press corps agree with James Fallows, a liberal analyst of the presidency who writes for the *Atlantic*. "Not even FDR was FDR at the start," Fallows wrote in a recent issue of the monthly magazine. "The evidence is that Obama is learning fast to use the tools of office."

Mainstream journalists contend that in the wake of the shellacking the Democrats took in the 2010 midterm elections, Obama & Co. were forced to go back to the drawing board.

According to this version of events, Obama and his political advisers concluded after the midterms that the president would lose in 2012 if the election were a referendum on the economy.* The election had to be a "choice election" between Obama and a "worse" Republican alternative in order for Obama to win, and he had to start beating up on his potential Republican opponent right away.

At this point, I can hear some readers interrupting. "We know where the liberal mainstream media stand," they might say. "Why should we care what they think?"

The answer is quite simple: the presidential nominee of the Republican Party will not only have to run against Barack Obama in 2012; he will also have to run against the full force and power of the liberal mainstream media and the cultural establishment. For all their carping about Obama's coldness, detachment, isolation, and grandiosity, and for all their disappointment over his failure to become a "transformative" president, mainstream journalists and their allies in the liberal establishment have never fallen out of love with Obama. They want to see Obama win in 2012. And their newest mantra is "Obama has grown in office."

Listen to what they have to say:

From the Washington bureau chief of a major city newspaper, who asked to remain anonymous: "Obama and his staff have

---

* Obama likes to boast that he has created more than 2 million jobs. But if he had matched Ronald Reagan's record, 15.7 million Americans would have been put to work.

learned a lot. They never saw the Tea Party thing coming. They were not nimble. They thought that Hillary Clinton had made a terrible mistake on the healthcare bill by sending a White House-created bill to Congress with a thousand-plus pages. So the Obama people decided not to send up a bill of their own. What's more, Obama was in favor of the public option. They knew it wasn't going to pass. The thought was he should have tried anyway. It would demonstrate to his base that he tried and that the votes weren't there. And the same people who didn't see the Tea Party coming, didn't see that a very complex proposal like ObamaCare needed to be explained in simple terms.

"Now, with a Republican-dominated House of Representatives, Obama and his staff have changed both strategy and tactics," this journalist continued. "They have a plan to put the onus on the Republicans. Rather than compromising from the start, as they did before, the president comes out and says, 'You want a definite deficit plan? Well, I've got one. And what are you going to do about it?' That is a big difference from the way they acted early on. They had to go through all of this to understand that the strategy of compromise wouldn't work."

And this from a White House correspondent: "There is plenty of evidence that Obama has grown in the job. The sharper the political knocks have become, the more he seems aware of his opponents. He's tried to be a nice guy. Now, he's picking a fight because the situation demands it and he has no choice. It's a Harry Truman strategy. His strategy is that he's the last sane man in Washington."

The notion that Obama has changed his stripes, that through trial and error he has become a better president, is now accepted as conventional wisdom inside the Washington Beltway. Indeed, Obama himself subscribes to this view; he even admits he's seen the error of his ways.

"While proud of his record, Obama has already begun thinking about what went wrong—and what he needs to do to change course…," Peter Baker wrote in the *New York Times*.

> He has spent what one aide called "a lot of time talking about Obama 2.0," with his new interim chief of staff, Pete Rouse, and his deputy chief of staff, Jim Messina. During our hour together, Obama told me he had no regrets about the broad direction of his presidency. But he did identify what he called "tactical lessons." He let himself look too much like "the same old tax-and-spend liberal Democrat." He realized too late that "there's no such thing as shovel-ready projects" when it comes to public works. Perhaps he should not have proposed tax breaks as part of his stimulus and instead "let the Republicans insist on the tax cuts" so it could be seen as a bipartisan compromise. Most of all, he has learned that, for all his anti-Washington rhetoric, he has to play by Washington rules if he wants to win in Washington.

All this talk about a "New Obama" reminds me of the effort on the part of Richard Nixon's PR people in the 1960s to repackage him as the "New Nixon." During the presidential election of 1968, voters were treated to TV commercials and carefully planted stories claiming that the old, mean-spirited Nixon had matured, and that a more tolerant, magnanimous "New Nixon" had taken his place. It was a brilliantly orchestrated campaign, but as we learned during Watergate and the subsequent release of Nixon's Oval Office tapes, there never was a "New Nixon."

The example of Richard Nixon's *non-makeover* makeover should tell us something about the efforts of the Obama political team to reframe his image and resell him to voters. The comparison between Nixon, the saturnine gutter fighter, and the No-Drama-Obama may strike some people as a stretch, but consider the following:

- Like Nixon, Obama is an introvert who prefers his own company to that of others
- Like Nixon, Obama has a frosty relationship with the press
- Like Nixon, Obama is thin-skinned and self-pitying
- Like Nixon, Obama relies on a tight inner circle of dedicated loyalists
- Like Nixon, Obama is a divisive political figure
- Like Nixon, Obama thinks anyone who disagrees with him is his sworn enemy and is out to destroy him

"Obama is among the most thin-skinned presidents we have had, and we see evidence of it in every possible venue imaginable, from one-on-one interviews to press conferences, from extemporaneous remarks to set speeches," says *Politics Daily* columnist Peter Wehner. "The president is constantly complaining about what others are saying about him. He is upset at Fox News, and conservative talk radio, and Republicans, and people carrying unflattering posters of him. He gets upset when his avalanche of faulty facts are challenged.... In Obama's eyes, he is always the aggrieved, always the violated, always the victim of some injustice. He is America's virtuous and valorous hero, a man of unusually pure motives and uncommon wisdom, under assault by the forces of darkness."

The comparison between Nixon and Obama is even more revealing when we consider how each of these presidents chose to sustain his political popularity. "Both men deployed populist-tinged, us-versus-them appeals," writes David O. Stewart, a constitutional lawyer and author of *American Emperor: Aaron Burr's Challenge to Jefferson's America.* "Nixon pronounced himself the choice of the 'silent majority' that supposedly supported the Vietnam War and disdained the era's counterculture. Expressing sympathy with the Occupy Wall Street movement, Obama has tried to identify himself as battling, on behalf of the nation, against the richest elites."

Those who claim there is a "New Obama" have invented a man who doesn't exist. Intentionally or not, they have conflated the president with the campaigner. The former has *not* changed: as president, Obama's ends and means remain the same; he is still governing from the Left. However, Obama-the-campaigner *has* adjusted his tactics, because his record in office will not carry him to victory in 2012.

If the notion of a "New Obama" turns out to be as fallacious as the notion of a "New Nixon" was more than forty years ago, that raises another question: What happened to the old Obama who was once hailed by liberals as their knight in shining armor and the country's savior? As I shall argue in the following chapter, *that* Obama was a total invention, too.

CHAPTER 21

IN SEARCH OF THE REAL OBAMA

What we've got here is a failure to communicate.

—Strother Martin in *Cool Hand Luke*

If Karl Rove was George W. Bush's architect, David Axelrod is Barack Obama's Homer.

A former newspaperman and Chicago-based political consultant, Axelrod is unmatched in his ability to help liberal candidates connect with voters through their personal stories. In the argot of Washington, Axelrod creates "narratives." Candidate Obama presented Axelrod with a unique challenge. Not only was Obama a black man in a country that had never sent an African-American to the White House, he also had the most liberal voting record in the United States Senate. Axelrod feared that Obama would come across as a threatening figure to white, mainstream voters.

To sell Obama to these voters, Axelrod performed a brilliant piece of political legerdemain. He turned Obama's negatives into positives. He devised a narrative for Obama in which the candidate was presented as a black man who would *heal* America, not *divide* it, a moderate nonpartisan who would *rescue* America, not *threaten* it. Axelrod sold Obama to a significant swath of the electorate as an American Messiah.

In Axelrod's narrative, Obama was a conciliator who had tried to bring together his white mother and black father, who strove to integrate the racial and cultural conflicts in his own life, who promised to heal the blue-state-red-state breach in America, and who vowed to rescue the world from all its ills.

"I am absolutely certain that generations from now," Obama declared during the 2008 campaign, sounding like King Canute holding back the tides of the sea, "we will be able to look back and tell our children that this was the moment when we began to provide care for the sick and good jobs to the jobless; this was the moment when the rise of the oceans began to slow and our planet began to heal; this was the moment when we ended a war and secured our nation and restored our image as the last, best hope on earth."

That Obama failed to deliver on such unrealistic promises did not come as a surprise to conservatives, who never bought into David Axelrod's fantasy that Obama was here to rescue us from our sins. But many influential people in the country's liberal establishment—people who run the media, publishing,

Hollywood, the music industry, fashion, certain mainstream Protestant denominations, and academia—swallowed the rescue fantasy hook, line, and sinker. It was David Axelrod's brilliant idea to market Obama to these "Influencers," who controlled the cultural megaphone and were in a position to spread the Gospel of Obama.

It is worth pointing out that when these members of the liberal establishment hailed Obama as the country's savior, they were indulging, as is their frequent habit, in a nasty form of reverse discrimination. In effect, they were saying that only a "super black" —a species of near-perfect humanity who was above reproach—was acceptable to white Americans, and that benighted African-Americans required a messiah to lead them out of the racial wasteland.

"The very idea that Obama should transform African Americans into the black Waltons is flawed," wrote *Time* magazine contributor Ta-Nehisi Coates.

> It rests on the notion that the black community, more than other communities, is characterized by a bunch of hapless layabouts who spend their days ticking off reparations demands and shaking their fist at the white man. The truth is that the dominant conversation in the black community today is not about racism or victimization but about self-improvement.... When Jesse Jackson claimed that Obama was "talking down to black people," there was no real rush among blacks to defend Jackson. That's because in terms of their

outlook, their belief in hard work and family, African Americans aren't any different from white Americans.

In any case, the media elevated Obama above the common herd and never properly vetted him. His record as a leftwing redistributionist was ignored. He got a free ride all the way to the White House. And a basic truth about Obama was largely underplayed and overlooked—namely, that Obama was the first Democratic presidential nominee to come from the left wing of his party since George McGovern ran against Richard Nixon in 1972.

In the thirty-six years since McGovern's doomed candidacy, the Democratic Party had fallen under the control of so-called centrist New Democrats like Bill Clinton, who had declared, "The era of big government is over." Obama was a throwback to New Deal big-government activism and federal intrusion into all aspects of American life. He represented a movement; he was the leader of a Leftwing Restoration.

If proof of this were needed, it came in January 2008 when Edward M. Kennedy endorsed Obama for president of the United States. As I wrote in my biography of Senator Kennedy, *Ted Kennedy: The Dream That Never Died*:

> Ted Kennedy saw himself as the guardian of liberal orthodoxy, the tribune of leftist interest groups—trade unions, feminists, environmentalists, teachers' unions, black activists—that defined the base of the Democratic Party. Ted believed that, after four decades of cautious-to-conservative administrations under both Republican

and Democratic presidents—Nixon, Ford, Carter, Reagan, Bush I, Clinton, and Bush II—the political pendulum was finally swinging back in *his* direction, from Right to Left, and that Barack Obama represented a once-in-a-generation opportunity to restore activist government as the country's dominant public philosophy.

As his last act before he died of brain cancer, Ted Kennedy—the Liberal Lion of the Senate who spent forty years pushing universal healthcare—passed the torch to Barack Obama. It is no exaggeration to say that practically every major measure proposed during Obama's four years in the White House flowed from that transaction, including ObamaCare, the preferential treatment of unions, the Dodd-Frank Wall Street Reform and Consumer Protection Act, and the veto of the Keystone XL Pipeline, to name just the most familiar. With Obama, America was in the hands of the most left-leaning president in its history.

All of which goes a long way toward explaining Barack Obama's mishandling of the economy.

Obama likes to remind his critics that he inherited the greatest financial crisis since the Great Depression from George W. Bush. True enough. But what he conveniently fails to mention is that his policies only made matters worse and prolonged America's suffering. Many reasons have been given for this failure, including the fact that Obama picked the wrong economic team. By choosing Timothy Geithner as Treasury Secretary, Lawrence Summers as director of the National Economic Council, Austan Goolsbee as chairman of the Council of Economic Advisers, and Melody Barnes as his chief domestic policy adviser, Obama stacked the deck with liberal neo-Keynesians who favored government activism over the private sector.

But there was a more basic reason for Obama's failure. He and his economic advisers ignored the lessons of history and were doomed to repeat the mistakes made by Franklin Roosevelt and his New Dealers in the 1930s.

As syndicated columnist Amity Shlaes points out in *The Forgotten Man*, her brilliant account of the Great Depression, liberals have embraced a flawed myth about Franklin Roosevelt's New Deal. They believe that "the economy of 1930 or 1931 could not revive without extensive intervention by Washington.... The same history teaches that the New Deal was the period in which Americans learned that government spending was important to recoveries; and that the consumer alone can solve the problem of 'excess capacity' on the producer's side."

Shlaes throws cold water on this liberal interpretation of the Great Depression. "The problem [with Roosevelt and his New Dealers]," she writes,

> was their naiveté about the economic value of Soviet-style or European-style collectivism—and the fact that they forced such collectivism upon their own country.... The *New Yorker* magazine's cartoons of the plump, terrified Wall Streeter were accurate; business was terrified of the president. But the cartoons did not

depict the consequences of that intimidation: that business decided to wait Roosevelt out, hold on to their cash, and invest in future years. Roosevelt retaliated by introducing a tax—the undistributed profits tax—to press the money out of them. Such forays prevented recovery and took the country into the depression within the Depression of 1937 and 1938.

Tax increases... intimidation of businessmen... massive new burdens on the economy—all of that happened eighty years ago. But there are eerie similarities between the New Deal, which failed to dig America out of the Great Depression, and the Obama administration's self-defeating efforts to stimulate the economy and end the Great Recession. Indeed, Obama's $800 billion neo-Keynesian stimulus package actually impeded economic recovery. According to John B. Taylor, a Stanford University economist who carried out an in-depth study of the stimulus, the government's spending did not result in growth and jobs.

"Individuals and families largely saved the transfers and tax rebates," Taylor wrote. "The federal government increased purchases, but by only an immaterial amount. State and local governments used the stimulus grants to reduce their net borrowing... rather than to increase expenditures, and they shifted expenditures away from purchases toward transfers. Some argue that the economy would have been worse off without these stimulus packages, but the results do not support that view."

When the economy did not respond to Obama's neo-Keynesian stimulus, and the "recovery summer" of 2010 failed to make an appearance, a desperate president looked around for someone to blame. He focused first on Republicans, whom he referred to as "obstructionists" and "enemies." David Plouffe, who served as Obama's 2008 campaign manager before he became his in-house political strategist, claimed that the president was fighting for the middle class, while the Republicans were bent on preserving tax breaks for millionaires, hedge fund operators, and corporations.

"The American people will have a choice [in 2012] about the direction they want to take the economy," Plouffe said. "Do they want, basically, a Gordon Gekko economy? Or do they want a president who says, 'Every decision I make is focused on the middle class?'"

When such populist poppycock didn't work, Obama looked elsewhere to cast blame. The economy wasn't responding because of the Japanese tsunami… or the Greek budget crisis… or the oil shock caused by the Arab spring… or anything but his administration's own misguided policies.

———————

Obama's own views about what he has—and has not—learned during his four years in the White House say a lot about why he has been such a failure as president.

"The area in my presidency where I think my management and understanding of the presidency evolved most," Obama has said, "and where I think we made the most mistakes, was less on the policy front and more on the communications front."

The communications front!

How could that be?

Didn't liberals hail Obama as the greatest communicator since Ronald Reagan?

And didn't Obama have an exalted opinion of his own oratorical skills? For instance, when Robert Marion Berry, a former Democratic congressman from Arkansas, warned Obama in 2010 that his leftwing policies could cause the Democrats to lose seats in the midterm election, just as such policies had under Clinton in 1994, the cocksure Obama replied, "Well, the big difference here and in '94 was you've got me."

Was it possible, then, that Obama was now falling back on the lame excuse: "What we have here is a failure to communicate"?

That was exactly what he was doing—and so were his cheerleaders on the Left. Take Frank Rich, the former columnist of the *New York Times*: "While perhaps no politician can ever duplicate Reagan's brand of sunny and homespun (if Hollywood-honed) geniality," Rich wrote, "Obama has his own radiance when he wants to turn it on.... But Obama is less adept at keeping his messages simple, consistent, and crystal-clear.... The pitch-perfect showmanship, timing and salesmanship... were in Reagan's résumé and bones. Obama doesn't have that training, but he was a great communicator when it came to selling his own story in the campaign, heaven knows. He has rarely rekindled that touch in the White House."

It was true that Obama, who had campaigned so effectively against Hillary Clinton and John McCain in 2008, had fumbled badly once he was in the White House. But the reason he lost his personal connection with the American people had little to do with his communication skills. It was not *how* he communicated, but *what* he communicated that lost him the affection of the country. The American people didn't care a fig about the *style* of Obama's message; they didn't like the *substance* of his message. He was just too liberal for America.

I once asked Ronald Reagan, after he had left the White House, whether he resented the people who charged that much of his public success was due to his skills as "the Great Communicator" rather than to the appeal of his political programs.

"I think there were other reasons for my effectiveness," Reagan told me. "I believe very deeply in the things I advocated in office. When I came into the White House, the previous administration was telling the people about how they were suffering from a malaise. I had the feeling that the American people were hungering for spiritual revival."

What's more, unlike Obama, Reagan enjoyed being president—and his joy was contagious. In fact, Reagan told me that he would have considered running for reelection in 1988, when he was nearly seventy-eight years old, if it hadn't been for the Twenty-second Amendment to the Constitution, limiting presidents to two terms in office.

"It was my own party, the Republican Party, that passed that amendment out of revenge for Roosevelt's four terms," he said. "But what that amendment is is an infringement on the democratic right of the people. The people have a right to vote for whomever they want and for as many times as they want."

The people also have a right to vote *against* a president who has failed them. The question is: Will they vote against Barack Obama in 2012?

CHAPTER 22

THE LOW ROAD

*I'm troubled by rhetoric that pits people
against each other.... We have never been a
nation of haves and have-nots. We are a nation
of haves and soon-to-haves, of people who
have made it and people who will make it.
And that's who we need to remain.*

—United States Senator Marco Rubio

To hear the candidates who run for president tell it, you'd think every election was an historic watershed. "This is the most important election in which you will ever have a chance to cast your vote," they tell us every four years. "This election will decide the course of politics for decades."

But most presidential elections are not watershed events. In point of fact, there have been only six such political realignments in American history, marking the end of one period and the beginning of another:

ER

- The election of 1800, in which Vice President Thomas Jefferson defeated President John Adams, who represented northern Federalist interests, and ushered in a generation of southern, agrarian-dominated Democratic-Republican Party rule
- The election of 1828, in which Andrew Jackson, the first president not born of privilege, defeated John Quincy Adams and solidified Democratic Party control
- The election of 1860, which brought Abraham Lincoln and the Republicans to the White House and unleashed the forces of the Civil War
- The election of 1896, in which Republican William McKinley defeated the populist Democrat William Jennings Bryan and set the United States on a course to become a world industrial power
- The election of 1932, in which Franklin Delano Roosevelt created the coalition that made the Democratic Party the dominant political force for almost fifty years
- The election of 1980, in which Ronald Reagan attracted working-class Democrats to his cause and launched a generation of conservatism

Will the election of 2012 usher in America's seventh political realignment?

A convincing argument can be made that it will. For the election will not only be a referendum on Barack Obama, the most liberal president this country has ever had, but it will also be a plebiscite on the future direction of America. If Obama is defeated, everything the Left stands for—universal healthcare, mandatory union membership, wealth distribution, a bigger and bigger federal government—will be defeated along with him. But if Obama wins, the Left will be entrenched for years to come, and the United States will continue its headlong rush toward a bloated, deficit-ridden entitlement state similar to those in Europe.

The election will present voters with a stark choice between a leftwing president who believes in engineering "the equality of outcome" and a conservative candidate who believes in the "equality of opportunity." A vote for Obama will be a vote in favor of an ever-larger role for the federal government to ensure so-called "fairness" in the system. A vote for the Republican candidate will be a vote for less government and greater individual freedom. Every indicator suggests that America is balanced between these two philosophies, and that the country could go either way.

"There is a genuinely interesting and important debate of ideas to be had over the size, reach, and role of the federal government in our lives," writes Peter Wehner. "Honorable people have very different views on this matter; some, like Obama, are drawn to a European-like model of social democracy, one that wants to centralize more and more power with the federal government as a means to eliminate income inequality and ensure greater fairness. Others believe the federal government has dramatically exceeded its constitutional authority, that it is leading us down a path to fiscal ruin, and in the process it is undermining civic character."

Obama does not want to engage in such a debate because he knows he will lose it. Over the past four years, the American people have become more conservative. According to a Gallup poll:

> Democrats have lost their solid political party affiliation advantage in 18 states since 2008, while Republicans have gained a solid advantage in 6 states.... The findings make it clear that U.S. states have undergone a dramatic political transformation since 2008, the year President Obama was elected, moving from a Democratically dominant political environment to one of parity.... Clearly, President Obama faces a much less favorable environment as he seeks a second term in office than he did when he was elected president.

And there is more bad news for Obama from the Gallup organization. According to a February 24, 2012, poll, a majority of Americans, 51 percent, say that Obama's political views are too liberal. "Americans' perception of Obama's ideology," says Gallup, "has changed significantly since he was elected. Four years ago, when Gallup first asked this question about Obama while he was competing for the 2008 Democratic presidential nomination, a plurality, 47 percent, thought his views were about right. At that time, 37 percent said his views were too liberal, compared with today's 51 percent."

Faced with these poll numbers, David Axelrod, Obama's political Merlin, has waved his magic wand again and conjured up a new persona for his candidate in 2012. Gone—*poof!*—is the American Messiah of 2008, who promised "hope and change." Gone—*poof!*—is the self-righteous figure who once proclaimed, "If you don't have any fresh ideas, then you use stale tactics to scare voters. If you don't have a record to run on, then you paint your opponent as someone people should run from." Gone—*poof!*—is Mr. Nice Guy.

Axelrod has ripped a page out of Harry Truman's 1948 playbook and fashioned a campaign for Obama in which he demonizes his opponents and runs against a "Do-Nothing" Republican Congress and its wealthy supporters. You can hear an echo of "Give 'em Hell Harry" when Obama declares: "This Congress—they are accustomed to doing nothing, and they're comfortable with doing nothing, and they keep on doing nothing." Or when he says, "My attitude is, get it done... [but] if they don't get it done, then we'll be running against a Congress that's not doing anything for the American people, and the choice will be very stark and will be very clear."

Axelrod's strategy is virtually a copy of a sixty-five-year-old memorandum written by Harry Truman's political guru, Clark Clifford, and titled "The Politics of 1948." The gist of Clifford's memo was the need to divert attention from Truman's domestic and foreign problems and make the contest a conflict between Congress and the president. In such a battle, Clifford argued,

"[t]he presidency is vastly more flexible than Congress.... There is little possibility that [the president] will get much cooperation from the Congress, but we want the president to be in a position to receive the credit for whatever they do accomplish while also being in a position to criticize the Congress for being obstructionists."

"It is obvious that Team Obama is deliberately following the Clark Clifford strategy," E. Michael Young wrote in *American Thinker*. "Like Truman, Obama called a special session of Congress to propose his American Jobs Act, knowing in advance that the Republican-controlled House would reject it. Like Truman, Obama used an executive order to effect social change in the military (by allowing gays to openly serve) to prop up his liberal base. And like Truman, Obama is giving speeches all around the country, saying the obstructionist 'do-nothing' Republicans in Congress are blocking his jobs bill, hurting the economy, and currying favor with the wealthy elites."

Axelrod's update of the Clifford strategy is aimed at solidifying the Democratic Party base, reclaiming the middle, and dividing the country through class warfare against "millionaires," "fat cats" and "the owners of yachts and corporate jets." There are, however, several problems with this approach. To begin with, despite the conventional wisdom, Truman's campaign against the Republicans in Congress was not the main factor in his come-from-behind victory against Republican Thomas Dewey in 1948. The economy had a lot more to do with it. The unemployment rate in 1947 and 1948 was a more than acceptable 3.5 percent, and the American economy was growing at a sizzling 6.8 percent in the first half of 1948. Compare that with Obama's situation

today, when unemployment is above 8 percent, and the economy is growing at an anemic 2 to 3 percent.

Second, in 1948, the Democratic Party was still the dominant force in American politics. Franklin Roosevelt was dead only three years, and many Americans still had fond memories of him and his New Deal. The Republicans, by contrast, were burdened by the albatross of "Hooverism"—a reputation for being indifferent to the plight of the poor and the struggling middle class. About 40 percent of the country identified with the Democrats back then. Today, only 33 percent identify as Democrats—and that number is declining all the time.

Third, "If Obama were a Republican, he could win with this sort of strategy: Repeat your party's most orthodox positions, and then rip your opponent to shreds," writes columnist David Brooks. "Republicans can win a contest between an orthodox Republican and an orthodox Democrat because they have the [mistrust] in government issue on their side. Democrats do not have that luxury. The party of [big] government cannot win an orthodox vs. orthodox campaign when [only] 15 percent of Americans trust government.... It's suicide."

Fourth, a strategy of class warfare threatens to damage the coalition that Obama put together in 2008. "The president won the lion's share of everyone making under $35,000," notes Mark Penn, a Democratic pollster.

> He then did very poorly with middle class voters, but he got a remarkable half of the 26 percent of voters whose households make over $100,000. Never before

have so many voters fallen into that category and never before had so many of them voted Democratic. Even [a majority of] the so-called top 1 percent making over $200,000… voted for Obama. Without similar support from those upper-income voters, Obama has no way to recreate the numbers that sailed him to victory.… What was so brilliant about the Obama 2008 election was that it brought together the upper and lower classes in a common mission of hope and change. Today, he is smashing apart that coalition.…

When voters are asked in 2012, "Are you better off today than you were four years ago?" they can give only one possible answer: "No!" Therefore, the only way Obama can win a second term in the White House is by diverting attention from his incompetence and sliming his Republican opponent.

"Over $15 trillion in debt," writes Joe Hagan in *New York Magazine*, "[more than 8] percent unemployment, yawning structural problems, a severely gridlocked government—Obama is in a box, and there is only one way out of this box: the low road."

Obama knows this, and he is gearing up for a campaign that will in no way resemble his inspirational "hope and change" campaign in 2008. This time around, his goal is to raise an overwhelming $1 billion campaign chest, unleash super-PACs backed by the unlimited financial resources of such leftwing billionaires as George Soros, and get down in the mud and wage the ugliest campaign in modern American history.

"It's a deeply pessimistic time," says Steve Schmidt, who served as senior strategist to the presidential campaign of Senator John McCain in 2008. "Neither party is talking honestly or directly about the country's problems and challenges. It's going to be an extremely mean-spirited campaign, filled with nonstop attack ads. The whole focus will be on disqualifying the alternative, not on the country's future. It will be very much the opposite of the hope-and-change theme of four years ago."

Obama's strategy will be to convince voters that *he* isn't the issue—that his Republican opponent is the issue—and that, as France's Louis XV famously said, "After me, the flood." The idea will be to frighten voters away from the "scary" Republican alternative.

"This is a choice about who we are and what we stand for," Obama declared, "and whoever wins this next election is going to set the template for this country for a long time to come.... The alternative I think is an approach to government that would fundamentally cripple America in meeting the challenges of the 21st Century."

Cripple America. Strong words that suggest a Republican president would devastate, ruin, and destroy the United States. One can just imagine David Axelrod sitting in his war room in Chicago and screening the infamous 1964 anti-Barry Goldwater TV commercial, which was created for President Lyndon Johnson by Tony Schwartz of Doyle Dane Bernbach, and which showed a little girl picking petals from a daisy while an ominous-sounding male voice counted down to the launch of a nuclear missile. As the camera slowly zoomed in, her eye was filled with an atomic mushroom cloud. The implication was that Goldwater would start a nuclear war and *cripple America*, destroy it. A voiceover from Johnson stated, "These are the stakes! To make a world in which all of God's children can live, or to go into the dark. We must love each other, or we must die." Then another voiceover, this one from sportscaster Chris Schenkel, said, "Vote for President Johnson on November 3. The stakes are too high for you to stay home."

It's a pretty safe bet that David Axelrod will try to devise an updated version of the "Daisy Girl" commercial in 2012, and that Barack Obama's mantra will be: *The stakes are too high for you to vote for that frightening Republican.*

"[Obama] is determined to make the election a contest between two policy alternatives, deliberately omitting the issue of competence," says Dick Morris. "He's like an incompetent employee hoping to save his job by advocating a broad-based shift in his corporation's philosophy in the hopes that his bosses will ignore his own poor performance."

———————

To win reelection in 2012, Barack Obama must divert the country's attention from his record of incompetence and amateurism. He doesn't want to remind people that America lost its triple-A credit rating on his watch—a downgrade that Republican Senator Lindsey Graham of South Carolina called a firing offense.

Republicans will have to remind them.

Obama doesn't want to remind people that he increased the national debt by nearly $5 trillion—the most rapid increase in debt under any president.

Republicans will have to remind them.

Obama doesn't want to remind people that he pushed through a bill that includes more than a trillion dollars in new healthcare spending and contains a 4.5 percent tax increase.

Republicans will have to remind them.

Obama doesn't want to remind people that Jon Corzine's bankrupt financial company, MF Global, which is under investigation by a grand jury for misusing clients' money, was one of the top sources of contributions to Obama's reelection campaign.

Republicans will have to remind them.

Obama doesn't want to remind people of his erratic stand on illegal immigration, which has swung wildly between fast-paced deportations—removing nearly 400,000 illegal foreigners in each of the last three years—to a policy of virtual amnesty.

Republicans will have to remind them.

Obama doesn't want to remind people of his inconsistency on environmental regulation—first pushing through burdensome, anti-business rules to toughen air-quality standards, then suddenly scrapping those rules to win over campaign supporters in the business community.

Republicans will have to remind them.

Obama doesn't want to remind people that he was for lower taxes before he was for higher taxes; that he was for forcing Catholic-affiliated institutions to provide contraceptive and abortion insurance before he was against forcing them to go against their religious principles; that he was for removing terrorists from Guantanamo before he was against it; that he was for bringing the country together before he was for dividing it; that he was for a grand bargain with the Republicans over the debt ceiling before he was against it; that he was for energy independence before he rejected the Keystone Pipeline; that he was in favor of extending an olive branch to the mullahs in Iran before he was against it....

Republicans will have to remind America that Barack Obama is The Amateur.

ACKNOWLEDGMENTS

One of the great pleasures of reporting a non-fiction book is that it forces you to get outside your zone of comfort. This is a good thing for a writer, for it compels you to do things you wouldn't ordinarily do—speak with strangers, make new friends, and renew forgotten acquaintances. Perhaps most important of all, it shakes you out of your intellectual complacency, and makes you re-examine your assumptions and justify your conclusions.

This is the eighth non-fiction book that I have written in the past sixteen years, and like all the rest, it has been a great tonic for the mind, body, and soul. The result is the book you hold in your hands, *The Amateur.* The yearlong project was an exhilarating experience that took me to more than a half dozen cities, either in person or by telephone or email. I now have the additional pleasure of acknowledging and thanking the people who helped me along the way.

In Chicago, I wish to thank Ali Abunimah, Laura Anderson, Richard Baehr, Douglas Baird, Joe Bast, Sherry Bender, Jeff Berkowitz, Robert Blackwell, Bill Brady, Senator Roland Burris, Charles Butler, Shael Cigal, Forrest Claypool, Delmarie Cobb, Rick Cohen, Drew Davis, Monique Davis, Kirk Dillard, Alan Dobry, Richard Epstein, Carol Felsenthal, Rhani Flowers, Dr. Ari Friedman, Dr. Arnold Goldberg, Martin Greene, Jack Guthman, Leslie Hairston, Hermene Hartman, Bill Higginson, Steve Huntley, the Reverend Jesse Jackson Sr., Thomas Jarrett, Emil Jones, John Kass, Jerry Kellman, Shalom Klein, Ed Lasky, Judith Lavin, Michael Lavin, Dave McKinney, David Mendell, Louis Meyers, James Montgomery, Joe Morris, Steve Nassiter, Abdon Pallasch, Alice Palmer, Father Michael Pfleger, Tom Peters, Joel Pollak, Toni Preckwinkle, Jack Roeser, Steve Rogers, Milt Rosenberg, Dr. David Scheiner, Paul Schmitz, Dan Shoman, Ira Silverstein, Dick Simpson, Tavis Smiley, Alan Solow, Joel Sprayregen, Bob Starks, Father Bill Stenzel, Don Terry, Charles Thomas, Betsey Thurman, Eric Voogd, Lee Walker, the Reverend Jeremiah Wright, and Jeri Wright.

In Washington, D.C., I wish to thank Harry Alford, Mike Allen, Jeff Bader, Admiral Denny Blair, Josh Block, Cassandra Butts, John Castellani, Anthony Cordesman, Robert Dallek, Dan Danner, Kenneth Duberstein, Douglas Feith, Don Fierce, Vince Frilici, Bill Harlow, Barry Jackson, George Little, Doug Lute, Clifford May, Mark McKinnon, Maureen Orth, Daniel Pipes, Joe

Pounder, Noam Scheiber, Bob Schieffer, Billy Tauzin, Jay Timmons, Armstrong Williams, and Sam Youngman.

In New York City, I wish to thank Walter Anderson, Sue Erikson Bloland, Dr. Robert Cancro, Sharon Churcher, Abe Foxman, Leslie Gelb, Ed Koch, John LeBoutillier, Ed Nardoza, Paxton Quigley, Brian Ross, Doug Schoen, and Liz Trotta.

In Boston, I wish to thank Bernard Cornwell, Nassir Ghaemi, Doris Kearns Goodwin, Elaine Kamarck, and Brian O'Connor.

In Florida, I wish to thank Steve Plamann and Chris Ruddy.

In Oregon, I wish to thank Richard Harmon and Courtney Hight.

In New Mexico, I wish to thank Joe Wilson.

In New Jersey, I wish to thank (ret.) Colonel Jack H. Jacobs.

In Honolulu, I wish to thank Henry Chapin.

I owe a special debt of gratitude to my longtime assistant, Leon Wagener, whose skills as an investigative reporter never cease to amaze. As in past books, Leon's reportorial gems are displayed in several key chapters.

At Regnery Publishing, I would like to single out Marji Ross, who was present at the creation—and evolution—of the project that turned into *The Amateur*. I should also like to thank Harry Crocker, who waited patiently for the completed manuscript, then shepherded it smartly and expertly to publication. I also want to thank Mary Beth Baker for her punctilious copy editing.

To Ryan Harbage, my agent, I am indebted for his handholding skills and his unflagging encouragement.

And then, of course, there is my wife, Dolores Barrett, about whom I cannot say enough, and therefore to whom I will only say, "I love you."

SOURCES

AUTHOR'S INTERVIEWS

Abdon Pallash, Alan Solow, Ali Abunimah, Armstrong Williams, Arnold Gold-berg, Barry Jackson, Bernard Cornwell, Beverly Berke, Bill Harlow, Bill Higginson, Bill Stenzel, Billy Tauzin, Bob Starks, Bradford Berenson, Brian O'Connor, Brian Ross, Carol Felsenthal, Charles Butler, Charles Thomas, Dan Danner, Daniel Borouchoff, Dave McKinney, David Mendell, David Scheiner, M.D., Delmarie Cobb, Don Fierce, Doris Kearns Goodwin, Douglas Baird, Douglas Feith, Drew Davis, Ed Lasky, Ed Nardoza, Edward Silverman, Elaine Kamarck, Elijah Zarlin, Forrest Claypool, Fred I. Greenstein, Henry Chapin, Harry Alford, Hermene Hartman, Ivby Brooks, Jack Guthman, Jack Jacobs, Jack Roeser, James Baker, James Montgomery, Jeff Bader, Jeff Berkowitz, Jeri Wright, the Reverend Jeremiah Wright, the Reverend Jesse Jackson, Jerry Kellman, Joe Bast, Joe Morris, Joe Pounder, Joel Pollak, Joel Sprayregen, Joel Weisman, John LeBoutillier, Josh Block, Judy Lavin, Kenneth Dubertein, Kirk Dillard, Laura Anderson, Lee Walker, Les Bond, Leslie Gelb, Leslie Hairston, Matt Kairis, Maureen Orth, Mike Flannery, Father Michael Pfleger, Nassir Gaemi, Paxton Quigley, Rabbi Samuel Gordon, Rahni Flowers, Richard Baehr, Richard Epstein, Richard Harmon, Rick Cohen, Robert Cancro, Roland Burris, Sam Youngman, Shael Cigal, Shalom Klein, Sharon Churcher, Steve Plamann, Steve Rogers, Sue Erikson Bloland, Tavis Smiley, Terry Martin, Thomas Jarrett, Timuel Black, Tom Peters, Toni Preckwinkle, Vince Frillici, Walter Anderson, William Cousins.

BIBLIOGRAPHY

Alter, Jonathan. *The Promise*. New York: Simon & Schuster, 2010.

Anderson, Christopher. *Barack and Michelle*. New York: William Morrow, 2009.

Betts, Kate. *Everyday Icon*. New York: Clarkson Potter, 2011.

Bloland, Sue Erikson. *In the Shadow of Fame*. New York: Penguin, 2006.

Campbell, Joseph. *The Hero with a Thousand Faces*. Novato: New World, 2008.

Cashill, Jack. *Deconstructing Obama*. New York: Threshold, 2011.

Codevila, Angelo M. *The Character of Nations*. New York: Basic, 2009.

———. *The Ruling Class*. New York: Beaufort, 2010.

Cohn, Norman. *The Pursuit of the Millennium*. New York: Oxford, 1970.

Corsi, Jerome R. *The Obama Nation*. New York: Pocket Star, 2088.

Dallek, Robert. *Hail to the Chief*. New York: Hyperion, 1996.

D'Souza, Dinish. *The Roots of Obama's Rage*. Washington, D.C.: Regnery, 2010.

Falk, Avner. *The Riddle of Barack Obama*. Santa Barbara: Praeger, 2010.

Feith, Douglas J. *War and Decision*. New York: Harper, 2008.

Frank, Justin A. *Obama on the Couch*. New York: Free Press, 2011.

Frazier, E. Franklin. *Black Bourgeoisie*. New York: Free Press, 1957.

Ghaemi, Nassir. *A First-Rate Madness*. New York: Penguin, 2011.

Goodwin, Doris Kearns. *No Ordinary Time*. New York: Simon & Schuster, 1994.

Greenstein, Fred I. *The Presidential Difference*. Princeton: Princeton, 2004.

Heilemann, John and Mark Halperin, *Game Change*. New York: Harper, 2010.

Jacobs, Ron. *Obamaland*. Honolulu: Trade, 2008.

Kennedy, Randall. *The Persistence of the Color Line*. New York: Pantheon, 2011.

Kissinger, Henry. *Diplomacy*. New York: Simon & Schuster, 1994.

Klein, Edward. *Ted Kennedy*. New York: Crown, 2009.

Kurtz, Stanley. *Radical-in-Chief*. New York: Threshold, 2010.

Lewis, Michael. *Boomerang*. New York: W. W. Norton, 2011.

Malkin, Michelle. *Culture of Corruption*. Washington, D.C.: Regnery, 2009.

Mendell, David. *Obama*. New York: Amistad, 2007.

Minnow, Martha. *Making All the Difference*. Ithaca: Cornell, 1990.

———. *In Brown's Wake*. Oxford: Oxford, 2010.

Mundy, Liza. *Michelle*. New York: Simon & Schuster, 2008.

Obama, Barack. *The Audacity of Hope*. New York: Vintage, 2006.

———. *Dreams from My Father*. New York: Three Rivers, 2004.

Rakove, Milton L. *We Don't Want Nobody Nobody Sent.* Bloomington: Indiana, 1979.

Remnick, David. *The Bridge.* New York: Vintage, 2011.

Robinson, Craig. *A Game of Character.* New York: Gotham, 2010.

Robinson, Eugene. *Disintegration.* New York: Doubleday, 2010.

Scott, Janny. *A Singular Woman.* New York: Riverhead, 2011.

Shlaes, Amity. *The Forgotten Man.* New York: Harper, 2007.

Steele, Shelby. *A Bound Man.* New York: Free Press, 2008.

Suskind, Ron. *Confidence Men.* New York: Harper, 2011.

Walker, Lee H. *Rediscovering Black Conservatism.* Chicago: Heartland, 2009.

Williams, Armstrong. *Reawakening Virtues.* Sarasota, Florida: New Chapter, 2011.

Wolffe, Richard. *Revival.* New York: Crown, 2010.

Woodward, Bob. *Obama's Wars.* New York: Simon & Schuster, 2010.

Wright, Jeremiah A. *A Sankofa Moment.* Dallas, Texas: Saint Paul, 2010.

INDEX